STAR ANCESTORS

STAR ANCESTORS

Extraterrestrial Contact
in the Native American Tradition

as spoken to

NANCY RED STAR

Bear & Company
Rochester, Vermont • Toronto, Canada

Bear & Company
One Park Street
Rochester, Vermont 05767
www.BearandCompanyBooks.com

Bear & Company is a division of Inner Traditions International

The Library of Congress has cataloged a previous edition of this book as follows:
Red Star, Nancy, 1950–
    Star ancestors : Indian wisdomkeepers share the teachings of the extraterrestrials / Nancy Red Star.
    p. cm.
    ISBN 0-89281-819-0
    1. Human-alien encounters—North America. 2. Indians of North America—Religion—Miscellanea. I. Title.
    BF2050 .R43 2000
    001.942—dc21
    00-022655

ISBN of current paperback edition: 978-1-59143-143-5

Printed and bound in India by Replika Press, Pvt. Ltd.

10 9 8 7 6 5 4 3

Text design and layout by Virginia Scott Bowman
This book was typeset in Garamond Premier Pro with Perpetua used as the display typeface

Frontmatter art:
page ii: Dzibilchaltún, Temple of the Seven Powers, photograph by Paul Duarte
page vi: *New Elder* by Huga (Joe Dana), Penobscot
page xi and xiii: *The Family* (details) by Alan Syliboy, Mi'kmaq

For the benefit of all sentient beings
And those who stand in the light of the awakening

In the reality of many realities
how we see what we see
affects the quality
of our reality

We are
children of earth and sky
DNA descendant and ancestor
human being physical spirit
bone flesh blood as spirit

We are
in time and space
but we're from beyond time and space
the past is part of the present
the future is part of the present
life and being are interwoven

We are
DNA of Earth, Moon, planets, stars
we are related to the universal
Creator created creation
spirit and intelligence with clarity
being and human as power

We are
a part of the memories of evolution
these memories carry knowledge
these memories carry our identity
beneath race, gender, class, age
beneath citizen, business, state, religion

We are human being
and these memories are trying
to remind us
human beings human beings
it is time to rise up,
remember who we are

JOHN TRUDELL

CONTENTS

ACKNOWLEDGMENTS

Thanks to:

My beloved mother, Joyce Burroughs Matthews, and Walter Jerome Matthews and John Burroughs, my great-grandfathers.

All the elders, young and old, who assisted me with interviews, love, and support.

My cousin, Shona Bear Clark.

My literary agent, William Gladstone; his family; and everyone at Waterside Productions.

My literary editors—Steven Fadden, Parvati Markus, and Marilyn M. Sorel.

The Ballantine family, especially Tad Wise.

My editors at Inner Traditions—Jon Graham and Susan Davidson.

My publisher in Germany, Wilhelm Heyne Verlag.

John Trudell, the Dawnland Center, Dana Pictou and Lorraine Landers, Robert Kennedy Jr., and friends of Bill W.

All who generously assisted me in the completion of my manuscript, including John Brower; Robin Easton; Mr. Kazi, former translator to the Dalai Lama; Cia and Roger Ricco; Armond Lara; Mali Keating and the Odanak family band; Edward C. Wolf; Dolly Leigh; Doris Minckler and her daughter, Mary Decarr.

All the artists who contributed their work, and photographers Alex Ward and Athi-Mara.

Graphic Impressions, for the printing of my hand-pulled caligraphs.

Tracy B. Terzi's library.

My students at Bard College, especially Lesley Kahn and Eric Landaverde.

Finally, many thanks to Chief Homer St. Francis and my family at the Sovereign Abenaki Nation of Missisquoi.

PREFACE

My name is Red Star. People will tell you that a red star is not a star at all, but a planet. My message is for this planet from other planets. Stars can take care of themselves.

I am not an elder. I am what is called a runner. I run between generations, sexes, cultures, and worlds. I run with mailbags full, gathering the rich oral traditions and images that detail Mesoamerican knowledge of our Star Ancestors. I gather the teachings of the past and present, and prophecies of the future.

Several years ago I was asked to document the extraterrestrial stories of indigenous peoples for a proposed rock concert in New Mexico, at the site of the Roswell UFO crash. Though the concert effort failed I continued to document Indian knowledge of our Star Ancestors and prophesy of their return—prophecies spoken thousands of years before such terms as *unidentified flying object* and *extraterrestrial* came into being.

◼ *Portrait of Nancy Red Star*
Peter Law, Northern Cheyenne

Our history with extraterrestrial life (or, as an elder corrected me, "ultraterrestrial" life) is of global significance at this time. Spiritual wisdomkeepers around the world have recognized signs that were predicted by the ancient prophecies. These signs have signified the Time Keepers that they must now speak their closely held sacred knowledge concerning our origin from the stars; the influence of visitation on the formation of culture, tradition, and ceremony; and the imminent return of our Star Guardians.

The Hopi call the world we are now in the Fifth World. The creation and destruction of four previous worlds is held in common belief by the Mayans, Tibetans, North American Indians, Egyptians, and other cultures around the world. In four previous worlds, on four previous continents, humankind held technology and rituals of the highest order. Now, in the Fifth World, the abuse of technology through greed has led us to chaos, a world out of balance with the natural laws. We are in the time of purification, the time between worlds, the time when we choose which path to walk. The emergence of peace is upon us. The hope for humanity lies in prayer and in returning to spiritual harmony with nature and humankind.

The people who follow the original instructions of our sky dieties will walk into the Sixth World. At the time of conquest the Sacred Hoop of Indian Nations was broken. Now the Indian peoples have regained their ceremonies, their languages, their songs and dances, uniting and mending Mesoamerica. With this healing the teachings return as an ancient text, a code of living to maintain the balance of Mother Earth. If we listen to the wisdomkeepers we will hear our instructions from our ancient guardians: the prayers, songs, and dances—the seeds. If we plant and caretake these seeds, the teachings will flourish. Should we trample them, disregard them—not nurture Earth—they will disintegrate by the wayside, and we with them.

These are *my* instructions: to find and pass on the traditions from the old ways. To protect the integrity of the oral tradition I did not pass this information through the wires—all interviews were written longhand. Following each interview in this book is a gift to the reader, a giveaway to keep the circle strong. May these gifts grow within your heart for the benefit of all living beings.

Soon I begin the second volume of *Star Ancestors,* completing my journey around the Hoop of Indian Nations. A runner never stops running, yet as I must run so I must sit to remember where my instructions are coming from, and send my prayers to that place.

The watchers, the guardians, walk with us. We will be visited by beings from outside this universe, as we always have. May we be ready to receive them.

1 WEAVING THE WEB IS THE WAY OF THE WOMEN

Caretaking the Planet

HARRIET GOODLUCK

> *They say they get abducted;*
> *We get visited.*
>
> JOSE LUCERO, SANTA CLARA PUEBLO

During the winter of 1996 Jose Lucero, my advisor for the Roswell documentary, passed to me an article from the Associated Press headlined "Navajo Flock to Home Visited By Tribal Gods" (May 29, 1996). Ninety-six-year-old Irene Yazzie, who hadn't spoken since she was struck by lightning years before, saw a light come down outside her hogan near Big Mountain and was unable to move. Two figures—one dressed in white, the other in blue—appeared before her. They demanded to know why the Navajo deities were no longer receiving prayers from the people. They assured her that dire consequences would fall within four years' time unless the Navajo people returned to their traditional ways.

The deities continued with instructions to conduct Corn Pollen prayers in the morning, and to use the Navajo language as the people had in the past. If they did not follow these directives, drought and other misfortunes would befall the people and the deities would not be able to intervene. Having delivered their warning, the two figures disappeared and left only a corn pollen outline of their footprints in a dusted circle.

Following the visitation Irene Yazzie found she could move again, and her ability to talk had returned.

Irene was told not to speak of the incident in any language other than Diné, and not to pass any discussion of what was revealed to her through the "electric wires." An interview with Irene Yazzie would not be possible; however, I had developed a close friendship with Harriet Goodluck, and she consented to interpret the message contained within the visit of the Navajo deities.

The interview with Harriet Goodluck was my first interview for *Star Ancestors*. I did not question that these deities may have been extraterrestrials, but accepted the information, as my own ancestors would have, with humility and gratitude.

We sat through the evening sharing tears on the pain and suffering of Mother Earth at this time. Harriet's reflections brought

◻ *Harriet Goodluck*
  Navajo Nation, New Mexico

childhood memories of a recurring dream. As I lay semiconscious, moving into a dream state, I would leave the small figure of my body below as I shot into the galaxy. Traveling through the darkness, the stars and planets passed me by. I voyaged ever deeper into a dark, sacred space. I was undisturbed, unafraid, until my travels would end, landing on earthly soil. Everywhere I looked and walked there was garbage; the land was contaminated with miles and miles of never-ending debris. Metal objects, glass, food, rubber—landfills full of discarded contaminants of modern civilization covering what had once been Earth. I had to walk through the endless path of toxic debris with no human life in sight. Then suddenly I was removed, finding myself traveling in a pure white light—the universe—traveling to eternity.

When I awoke, I would be frightened by what the world would become. —NRS

Harriet Goodluck is an eighty-one-year-old full-blooded Diné (Navajo) woman. She has spent most of her life in the Four Corners of the Southwest and is fluent in Diné. Long married to a traditional Diné man, she is mother to eight children, grandmother to thirty, and great-grandmother to eleven. Harriet worked as a registered nurse and is now retired on her farm, where she has fruit trees, corn, alfalfa, and herds of cattle and sheep.

Thank you for the tobacco from the Clan Mothers at Onondaga, New York! Your telephone call and this visit are the answer to my prayers. Ever since Irene Yazzie's sighting I knew the time was close, and I wanted to speak on this. My husband is traditional; he speaks only Diné, and would not speak of the incident. Irene was told by the deities not to pass word of the visit through the electric wires, and only to pass word of it mouth to mouth. The only reason I can talk to you is because I walk in both worlds. I heard of the visit not too long ago. I heard through the grapevine that there was a lot of secrecy surrounding the contact. Because of the secrecy, the sacredness, I did not want to know any more.

This visit was a warning to the Navajo people, a reminder from the gods to once again honor our ways and traditions: the Corn Pollen prayers, the ceremonies, the songs and dances. Unless we do this, and do this with our young, we will have major disasters; the Navajo deities will not be able to help us unless we give them power with our prayers. This instruction also came through the visit: we must share the land that we have together with the Hopi. We don't have much time—the deities warn that we have four years. Now Irene Yazzie speaks after years of silence—since she was struck by lightning and suffered a stroke. The visitors left two sets of footprints inside a circle at Irene's hogan, a Navajo hogan on Hopi land. It is the Holy People.

The deities are foretelling what will happen in the next four years. Soon the boiling turmoil of the world will burst in fire or water. Even the archaeologists and environmentalists, people who study the origin of nature, are, whether they know it or not, beginning to see what Indian people believe. We are now coming to another creation. NASA sent a recording of the Yei-bih-chai, the Night Chant, on the Voyager 1 spacecraft in 1977, in an attempt to make contact with extraterrestrial life. They sent the chant out on sound waves. Some Navajos disagreed with sending the chant. They say originally the Twin Brothers had gone into space on the light, on the colors of the rainbow. In those days the Twin Brothers went to receive a message for saving the people down here. Now Irene Yazzie has been visited by Talking God and the Water Bearer—one dressed in blue and one dressed in white. The message is to return to the spiritual way of life.

The world is divided into four. We call these worlds Mother Earth

(Nahas-tsan beh-assun), Father Sky (Yaah-diklith beh-hasteen), Holy Water (Toho), and Fire God (Hashjesh-jin). Scientists are now finding out that there are Earths up in the heavens. When explorations return to Earth scientists discover that there are living things in the sky.

When this world started it was the end of another world. The world originated from up there and is now here. Earth is still alive and Water is still making it live. We are all circled together. If you sit here and watch the worlds you can see why the Indian people call the worlds Earth Mother, Father Sky, Fire God, and Holy Water. Like before, people will return to the path of the underworld. All of life goes back up into a world far ahead of us. The balls of stars, the comets, are living messengers.

Corn is the original food, the food of creation. The Pollen Road is the road of creation—the creation of plants, of bird life, of all life. All the prayers that the Navajo say are about corn pollen. Tha-dih-dean is the Corn Pollen Prayer of creation. Tha-dih-dean is used in all the ceremonies—for marriage, for sickness, in Blessing Way songs, in the Night Chant. We use this phrase in every prayer—for evening, for thanksgiving, for blessing anything. The sacredness of the prayers is taught to us in a very reverent manner.

This is called the Corn Pollen Prayer. This is what it is used for; this is how it is used.

I have corn pollen here; I make my own. Corn pollen is sacred; you should have it all the time. It protects you from natural disasters. I gather my corn pollen from the fields, early in the morning before the Sun comes up, when it's just dawn. Sometimes it is cold. Sometimes it is warm. You get your baskets and you put your cloth in it. You say your prayers before you go, prayers to the Tha-dih-dean. The prayers ask, "Lead me on the path of the corn pollen. Lead me to the end of it," which means to old age.

You gather the corn pollen when the tassels grow. The corn husks don't open until the bells themselves, the tassels, show. You will know; the pollen will show on the corn husks. When the leaves come out the pollen will show on the creases. You have to watch carefully; you have to check all the time. The bees will come around. It's early in the cycle of the corn, when the fibers of the corn start to arrive. The corn pollen drops on the fibers to germinate them. If you wait too long and the wind blows, you miss it.

At this point Harriet stood up, her corn pollen pouch cupped in her right hand. Her pouch is a beautiful white doeskin bag, beaded around the edges, each bead representing a prayer. She licked her left index finger and placed it inside the bag, returning with yellow powder that she placed on her tongue and upon the crown of her head. Facing east, she held her hand upward, giving a prayer. She proceeded to turn to each of the four directions. She held out the pollen bag to me. I followed her instructions.

"Dear Mother, I am going into your hand for you to give me your life light. I want you to help me, to give to me all you can give to me today, and I will thank you."

After her prayer, Harriet instructed me in collecting the corn pollen.

The women sing the songs for the corn. You bend the corn stalks and shake them. The pollen comes off the stalk. You can see it come down early in the morning when there is no wind. You collect as much as you can until the Sun comes up. Then the wind begins blowing, so you fold the cloth and go in.

You have to let the corn pollen dry. All of the bugs will die out. Some of them will just step away by themselves; others have to be picked out of the pollen. Some of them you can barely see. Some are light green; some are yellow, like the pollen, with little tiny wings.

When the corn pollen is dry I put it in a jar. I always keep some in my doeskin pouch. You lick your finger to make it wet, then reach into the pouch. Put some corn pollen in your mouth and on the crown of your head; the corn pollen is sweet. Any that is left over you put toward the Sun, always toward the Sun. East, south, west, north: everything is four ways.

I'm a full-blooded Navajo woman and I go to church. I was raised

▣ *Grandmother and
her Grandaughter*
Armond Lara, Navajo

all my life in the mission; I was in the boarding schools since the age of four-and-a-half. These ceremonies are becoming memories of our past. As much as I can't write the language of my native tongue or tell you understandably in Navajo, I can recall the past in my adopted tongue, English. I regret to say that in many Navajo homes all over the reservation this is the case.

My first memory is like a dream upon awakening. I see my mother. She was a tall lady with not very dark hair, somewhat lighter than black. The relatives around us called her Tall Lady or, in Navajo, "Uszannez." I remember having one brother and a sister. Somehow we were always left at home or with relatives. My mother would have the medicine man come to sing over her or pray for her. In Navajo the word for a medicine man who prays or sings over someone is *ha talle.*

The Hozhoni songs are songs given to us by the gods. If there was a sickness somewhere people would talk about it. They would say the sickness was caused by lightning, and they would find a person who specialized in lightning-struck songs or prayers. Sometimes a person became sick from shaking hands with a werewolf, a person who is a devil and yet is alive like you and me. At night that person

changes into a werewolf, or worse. These people run all over the reservation digging up graves, stealing the jewelry from graves or even from homes. Then they change back into a real person. Contact with them can bring on sickness. People still say this happens; they talk about it and I listen.

Another person might need a Nine-Day Chant because of illness. There may be another person who is bewitched by some animosity between himself and the White man. The White man could be a German or a Mormon or a cop [government agent] who causes him to be sick. There is a medicine man who specializes in prayers to ward off such sickness.

I discovered at the age of ten that I had a father somewhere else. His name was John Morgan. He was a full-blooded Navajo. John Morgan—that name, like so many others, was given by the government. There's a man right up the road here whose name is Woodrow Wilson. A man named Waldo Emerson still lives up the road, and a General Miles. That's what they did to the people. See, the government schools were started in the early 1900s. At that time all the children had Navajo names, of course, names which no one from the outside could pronounce. So my dad's name became John Morgan.

My husband's name is Goodluck—that name goes back to his great-grandfather. The railroad people took him out to California because he was an excellent silversmith. He went with the Santa Fe Railroad. They used to say, "Oh, he's a good-looking chap; he's a good-looking guy." Good looking. Goodluck. That's how he got the name.

I realize now that my mother was not at all healthy. She used to say that we should all go to school and get an education because she wasn't going to live very long. When spoken in Navajo this statement means a lot to me, even to this day. My mother suffered from tuberculosis, a very complicated sickness that none of the Indians who specialized in illness could comprehend. I know now that they were puzzled by the germs and diseases that caused so many deaths.

On my three months off from mission school, when my mother

was still alive, we would travel on the Santa Fe Railroad. My mother wove very beautiful rugs. She and other Navajo women from the area would weave rugs to sell, and then we had a lot more to eat. We could even bring food to some of our relatives who had asked for help. Sometimes I wondered why my father did not give us some of his land; we could have had some sheep to care for. A lot of Navajo families made a pretty good income from wool and the sale of lambs. I guess he was too busy keeping up with the automobile, keeping up with the Joneses! *[Laughs.]* We were struggling with survival, but he never interfered in our poverty.

My mother died at the age of thirty-four, at the Fort Defiance Hospital. She died of the tuberculosis. At school break we were taken to my aunt. My brother and sister and I lived in a one-room hogan. There was a small tent in the sheep corral nearby. An orphan boy lived in the tent and tended the sheep. We did not call him by his name; we all called him "my brother."

Living with my aunt in that strange place, where I never was before, I longed for the mountains. There were plenty of mountains where we were. When we traveled we camped along the way at different places where we could find abandoned sheep corrals for our small herd to stay overnight. Our little wagon was overflowing and we traveled a long way. My aunt would make rugs along the way to trade for food. Girls my age made rugs alongside their mothers. They would take them to the trading post to reclaim their pawn, or to buy some new material for clothes, or maybe buy shoes to go to the Indian school or Indian dances.

During plowing time or planting time we had many relatives come to help. They would tease and laugh and we all would have a lot of fun. During those days we had plenty of meat and home-baked bread. A lot of women would cook for the workers. We worked from a little after sunup until sundown, till all the corn and melon were planted. Sometimes we were fortunate to plant some pinto beans if the ground was wet. We did not know the art of farming but we depended on the good rain. The rain came more often in those days. Even without rain we used to have a lot of corn and melons at harvesttime. My mother always told me to put six or seven seeds into the ground. She said if we did that we would carry six or seven loads of corn at harvesttime, or six or seven loads of each crop. I believed her. Even to this day, when it comes to planting corn, watermelon, or pumpkin, I still put six seeds into the ground.

We moved from place to place to place. Every time I came home from the mission school we were in a different place. It was always near a water hole or pond. These small ponds had timber and trees around them. We climbed the juniper trees because they were flexible and long. We used to ride on the branches. One of us would jump up and down and the other would hold the branch's end. When we would get hungry from all that playing we would corner some nanny goat in the creek and take turns sucking the warm milk.

All we had then were government-issued tennis shoes made out of heavy canvas, with rubberized soles. All the Navajos called them "sticky shoes" because, no matter how new they were, when you went outside you always got stickers on your shoes. The burrs would just stick to the canvas, and you could not escape a cactus. You would always be worse off than when you left home; in the evening you had to take all the stickers off your feet.

In those days we had to carry wood and water. We had two long, straight pieces of wood that each of us held in our hands. We put the rest of the wood crosswise on top of those pieces. This would make quite a pile. That is how we carried wood home. We had a small water hole fed by a stream that came from the hills above us. We had to walk quite a ways by ourselves carrying a small wooden keg that was strapped around the chest, or sometimes around the head. You couldn't put the keg down for a rest if you were alone. Once you started home with that thing on your back you had to keep going.

The last time I saw my aunt we went to a Yei-bih-chai. It was a big ceremony, the Nine-Night Chant. We stayed the whole time. I was wearing my Indian clothes for ceremony. The last night she covered me up and put on my other clothing, my new school clothes. She took me back to the mission school after the ceremony. My aunt passed on from depression. She took her life.

I still attend Christian church, but I practice the ways of my people. I pray in Navajo. I grow and harvest my own corn pollen. I do both, Christian and Navajo. That is my way. I made a promise to Pope John Paul that I would say the rosary every night. That is a spiritual promise.

I see what is happening in the world and I fear for the children. I see the droughts and more Earth upheaval coming if we do not return to our traditional language and Corn Pollen prayers. The children, however, don't want to speak the language. They don't want the ceremony. They want the fast life to nowhere—alcohol, drugs, fast cars, loud music, TV, violence. This is not the Navajo way. I tell them but they don't listen. That's what scares me! They don't listen to their elders.

I went down to the chapter house, the community center, yesterday morning. There was a crowd of cars and I wanted to know what was happening. One woman was yelling and screaming, cutting down all the progress the people are trying to make. This was a meeting about domestic violence. As soon as I hear her screaming about domestic violence it came to me that the whole world, this whole universe, is in a state of domestic violence—the guns, the tanks, the bombs, the pleading, the prayers. Civilization brought the violence of today. The modernization of this world has spoiled everything. The technology and the greed for money—those are the first things modern man goes for. A poor person isn't human to most people. You have to be rich—a rich human being is power. However, people can live their entire lives in poverty and live as long as they can, just living in the world with nothing. To me they are living the spiritual life because, even if they don't have anything to eat, they will pray. What is there to stop them from praying?

All I say is that our reservation is going nowhere spiritually. All the money won't protect us from the storms, the floods, the earthquakes, the tornadoes, the drought. We sit and pray that it should not happen here. The only belief, the tiny belief, that older people have they are instilling in the young ones. "Mom, why is it flooding there? Grandma, look another storm—why doesn't it rain here?" "Well, baby, we have the sacred mountains to protect us."

Spiritually the Four Corners is a protected area, and leads us back to the prayers. So I will continue to talk to the young people, even if they do not listen. I will not stop. I will do my traditional Navajo prayers and I will attend church. I will watch the Earth and I will know by how she speaks. I will pray for rain, and see if there is rain. I will watch other places in the world and I will know how much pain Mother Earth is in. I will always talk to my people so they can heed the warning from our Navajo Holy People. I'll follow what the old people still believe in—the prayers, the offerings, the ceremony, and the giving of something to the Holy People.

CARETAKING THE PLANET

Mirror a Portrait Of Mother Earth A canvas painted with nourishment Brushes dancing among wild-crafted gardens Spinning yarns of color Pallets of birth and death A blood moon Casts the threads of seasons Cycles to blanket our Mother Earth Weaving a dance Of lights and shadows Is the way of women Corn Mother and her grandchildren Corn Mother and her great-grandchildren

Walking the pollen road The road of creation Hear her as she walks by you now Riding on her yellow powder Through the wind Her skirt tails flying Songs and chants Echo breaths of life Breathing prayers Meet her at sunup Call to her a chant A ceremony of songs A prayer for her Creating a blessing for you

Ask her for what you take Give her your breath Breath of Life Blood memories To honor our Star Ancestors Always coming home To caretake the planet In her moment of dawn She calls to you For ears of corn She lends the good rain Creates a new world Born for you

The three sisters Ancient midwives Corn Beans Squash Sister foods of life Venus love For the cosmic human Music of Earth Mother cycling her axis Moon revolving around her Mother Earth orbiting Sky Father The round dance Of day and night Playing rhythms Circling the spheres Sounding within you Sing a song for her Say a prayer of thanks

2 VISIONS OF A RED ROAD WARRIOR

Principles of Red Road Recovery

DANA PICTOU

> *If you have a way to spread the truth, through the newspapers, radio, books, through meetings with powerful people, tell the truth!*
>
> *Tell them what you know to be true.*
>
> *Tell them what you have seen here; what you have heard us say; what you have seen with your own eyes.*
>
> *In this way, if we do fail, let it be said that we tried, right up to the end, to hold fast to the path of peace as we were originally instructed to do by the Great Spirit.*
>
> *Should you really succeed, we will all realize our mistakes of the past and return to the true path—living in harmony as brothers and sisters, sharing our Mother, the Earth, with all other living creatures.*
>
> *In this way, we could bring about a new world!*
>
> DAN EVEHEMA, ELDEST ELDER
> HOPI SOVEREIGN NATION

Soon after returning home from my visit with Harriet Goodluck, my involvement with the Roswell concert ended. In those months I had developed film scripts for a global telecast documenting the "Sky Elder" theme found in virtually every indigenous culture. The prophecies gathered pointed to humanity's ultimate responsibility for the Blue Star (Earth), and gave instructions guiding humanity's relations with the laws of Mother Nature.

I could not give up the purpose of gathering these original instructions, which caused me to deeply question the course of my life. It was at this turning point that I found a most amazing rock: a rock with two eyes and no mouth, only a telepathic funnel on top of the "head." It was a talking rock.

I recognized the significance of this gift. The face belongs to the Little People, and I knew when I found this rock that my journey was being guided by these telepathic beings.

I had been clean and sober for over a decade when I met Dana Pictou at the Dawnland Center's Red Road meetings. My interview with Dana, in which I learned about the Mi'kMaq "Little Boy" rocks, confirmed that my journey would continue to be safely guided.

The Dawnland Center follows the teachings of community healing for the purpose of recovery from all forms of addiction and trauma. The focus is on the strengths and healthy sources of encouragement that historically have been available to Indian people. The community healing work fosters a sense of purpose and a knowledge of what it means to serve the Greater Good. It is a method of promoting healthy lifeways and well-being. When we are in circles together we are reminded of the need to be grateful and to place highest regard on the work that is done to uphold the Greater Good. We have a personal regard to honor the legacy of the teachings and the Star Ancestors, hoping that all our dances

■ *Dana Pictou*
  Mi'kmaq, Nova Scotia

and songs will be the walking prayers for the continued healing of the Blue Star. The Eastern people have begun again to live in the joy of the Dawnland. The message presents a ray of hope that humanity will heed the words of the spiritual leaders and help bring about the passage from the Fourth World to an era of peace in the Fifth World. —NRS

Dana Pictou is a member of the Acadia Band of the Mi'kmaq in Nova Scotia. Born of the Turtle Clan, Dana is a traditional ash-basket maker, and teacher of that art. He served on the board of directors for the Rhode Island Indian Council in the 1990s developed the Shooting Star Lodge, an intertribal education outreach program. While earning a master of science degree in psychology, he and his wife, Lorraine Landers, started the Dawnland Center for alcohol and drug recovery—what is known among the Indians as Red Road work.

Father of three and grandfather of three, Dana lives in the backwoods of Vermont with his wife. They own a thirty-five-acre farm complete with a medicine lodge, a longhouse, and a women's house. Together they raise wild turkeys, corn, beans, squash, and Penobscot pumpkin.

K *we Kwe* (greetings) Star Ancestors.
See, among the Mi'kmaq, the Little People are believed to be alive in spirit on islands in Nova Scotia and Maine. It's said you can find these beings in rocks that have all these little holes in them. You make necklaces out of the rocks. Only very special people find these rocks. The holes are not natural; they're carved. The Little People carve them and leave them for those who come into their circle during a

◨ *Talking Rock*
Alex Ward

vision time. It's then that you're visited by a Little Person. You won't even know that they were there, but they leave you something.

At my vision time I cleared a piece of earth—cleared it of all that was standing and rooted and half-buried in the ground. I made sure it was smooth and there wasn't anything impure in that little circle of earth. After my vision time was over I found this little stone with a hole in it. I put it in my bag and showed the elder who was helping me to the vision. He said, "Well, you got visited by the Little People."

As a child I learned the Mi'kmaq songs about the Little People sitting on a high hill, singing out to others who are coming in from across the ocean. One is called Kwedun Uktabegeakun, the Canoe Song. The Little People sing us safely to shore. The Little People have always been guides for the Mi'kmaq.

I was standing in the vision circle for the second night, gazing into the south. This was my rite of passage, guided by my teacher and grandfather, Wayindaga. He was Nanicoki (Delaware Indian). I was looking into the south; it was two or three o'clock in the morning. I was having a lot of visions. I saw these lights like comets coming down from the sky. Then they would stop, and I could see Little People dropping from the sky in the distance, just far enough so I couldn't make them out once they reached the ground. Then they would come running out of the woods. I tried to look without blinking to make sure I wasn't "seeing" things. When I would look up I would see them dropping from the sky again. This lasted for forty-five minutes or an hour, Little People just dropping from the sky. I was looking to see where they landed, but I couldn't find the place.

That morning, after daylight, I found the rock. That was after thirty-two months of sobriety. It was 1991 when I went up there on the mountain. I have never talked about this before. You're not supposed to give out your visions.

In the past there was always such talk, but only Indian to Indian. I remember as a little boy my grandfather told me that he talked to some elders when he was very young. Now, my grandfather was born in 1910, so he was talking to elders born in 1860 or 1870. One of the elders many times told my grandfather that travel-in-the-sky was going to happen in the very near future. My grandfather would ask him how he knew and the elder would say, "Because I've seen things flying through the sky." My grandfather was very sincere about that, and the elder was very sincere about what he was telling. Grandfather wanted my father to tell other people that these things were going to happen.

I remember in the blueberry fields listening to the elders. They would tell you stories of the visitors: seeing Woman-in-the-Sky, who they had been visited by; a flash that wasn't a plane or rocket or satellite. They got you to understand that we were not the only people around. There are other beings—guides who gift only a few special folk. That was always something I had in the back of my head.

Once in Wisconsin I cleared a whole area of grass to make a fire. Out there they have what are called "Little Boys." I'll show you the one I keep in my bundle.

Two Sisters

 Two Sisters
Alan Syliboy, Mi'kmaq

At this time Dana stood up and got his bundle. As he approached he opened a deerskin pouch and withdrew a Little Boy, which I held in my hands.

I cleaned up this whole area to build a fire. The next morning, before we went to ceremony, I patted the fire to make sure there were no hot coals and I found this great big rock. I wondered just how it had gotten in there. I knew that I had cleaned the whole area to make sure there were no rocks, and that nobody had thrown anything in there because that was our fire that we had put our tobacco in, first thing in the morning. The next thing I knew there was another elder patting around the ashes of the fire to find another stone. *[Laughs.]* He couldn't find one.

Now, with the prophecy unfolding, the time for secrets is over. It is through my vision of the Little People that I received my instructions to do the Red Road work, and it's how I got my spirit name, the one I use in ceremony. It was after my initiation experience; grandfather was getting ready to take me into the lodge, but first he wanted to know what was the most important thing I saw. He said, "What was the most vivid thing? Because this is where you are going to get your name." I told him, and from that he named me Shooting Star—Seeker of Vision. In Mi'kmaq it's Teemeidas Kulokowedj.

To me, Little People are Spirit People. I explained to grandfather how the Little People were coming down in different colors, then they would hit the treetops and I couldn't see them anymore. I would be looking, searching for them. What I gathered from that was I needed to make the place where they land more real. I needed to do the Red Road work. The Red Road is where visions meet the planet, where spirit meets dirt. It's about purifying ourselves. On the practical side, Red Road work is all about alcoholism, drug addiction, and community healing, about living as a bicultural warrior in today's society. It's about staying with the old ways but also integrating into the white governmental society.

I guess that was the purpose of the Little People's visit, to show me that I could live a sober life and still experience the vision state. The big thing was doing the work—using the teachings and traditions to help other people get sober. Native people today want their people to be sober; they want everybody to be sober by the year 2000 in preparation for the Earth changes. In trying to tell people about what's going to happen they may not believe us, but at least we won't give them the excuse of us being drunk or high on drugs. If people aren't ready—for the ancestors to come, for the unfolding of the prophecy, for the path of survival and the path of destruction—if they aren't ready they won't survive the change.

Sometime around 1980, when I was still living on the reservation, my brother-in-law and I were out jacking deer. We were in a field;

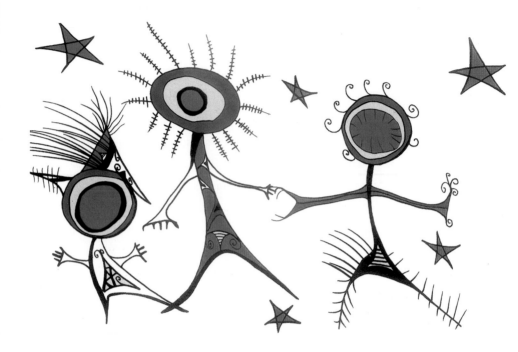

◼ *The Family*
Alan Syliboy, Mi'kmaq

it was November, around seven or eight o'clock at night. We weren't drinking at that time. We never drank when we jacked deer—we only drank after we got back home. We were sitting underneath a bunch of spruces; we had our apples at the other end of the field, waiting for the deer to come in. Off in the east we saw something in the sky, moving fast. "Is that a plane?" I asked. No, it wasn't a plane; it was moving too fast. Then we thought it might be a satellite, but the craft was moving too fast, maybe six or seven hundred miles an hour across the sky. When it reached us it stopped.

The craft hovered right over us and to the north a little bit, as if over the Yarmouth area, near the Bay of Fundy. It had lights on the bottom, moving around in a circle. Through the scope on my gun I could see that the craft was huge. I knew it wasn't a plane. I thought, "Nobody is going to believe us, that we watched this."

The craft stayed there for about fifteen minutes, then suddently it was gone, out of sight. We did not even know if it flew straight up or at an angle. When it decided to leave it was just gone.

When we went back to the house my wife thought we were stoned or drunk, so we each sat down and drew a picture of what we saw. We put both pictures together and they were identical. We knew what we had seen.

We told other people on the reservation and everyone began saying, "Dana and Joe must be having d.t.'s or hallucinations from LSD." Nobody believed that we saw what we saw. There were, however, other people in the Yarmouth area who claimed to have seen the craft. I don't know if it's in the records or not, but I know what I saw.

When I was in the Navy we went through the Bermuda Triangle. To get to Guantánamo Bay you had to go through the Triangle. I was doing a lot of drinking at the time and had a lot of drugs on the boat. The captain would get upset because I wouldn't pay much attention when we passed through the Triangle—I used to move the captain's hat or hide someone's binoculars. I did not really believe in the Triangle itself. When the captains, lieutenants, and officers would go through the Triangle they were full of fear. That was true for every ship and every airplane that passed through this area. They were afraid the ship would disappear or that something unknown would appear. The captains and the officers were always on edge. There have been planes missing in that area, boats missing in that area. Ships being towed have suddenly disappeared.

I always made it through the Triangle, but now I believe there are other beings out there. I want to be beamed up! If they are going to come, let them come and take me away. I'd be happy to go! It all comes back to standing in the circle for my vision, my passage of rites. I learned then what I needed to do to prepare for their return.

Yes, it's preparation time. Talk to the grandparents. Grandfather was a strong believer. He told us that if we were going to do any kind of work we had to get away from the ocean, that we had to live in the

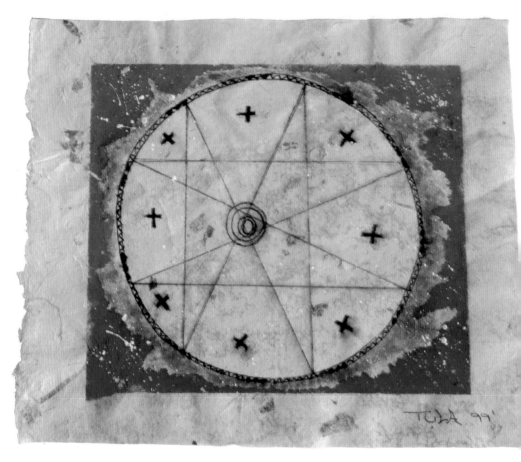

▣ *Na'Ku'Set (Sun, Giver of Life)*
  Tula, Abenaki/Cherokee

mountains because the coastline was going to be flooded. The people
who were to be saved were in the mountains. So we all said we'd do
as he said. He was in the Allegheny Mountains in Pennsylvania. He
wanted to set up places to get people sober, to help Indians get on the
Red Road, to live in the traditions and spiritual life that we're meant
to be living. That's why I started the Dawnland Center—to honor my
grandfather and his grandfather, and the prophecy they lived by.

I don't feel that I need to seek another vision. I battled myself and
I killed the old way—my alcoholism—to live in a healthier traditional
way. I believe I was visited by many, many spirits, and that I will meet

them again. When I found that rock from the Little People, coming on dawn, I knew my life was changed, that I had to go back to the old way of life, of listening to elders. My grandfather's very last wish, after he had a stroke, was that I get off the reservation. He said that it was no place for me. I listened to him. I got off the reservation and I got sober.

The elder who took me through rites of passage for vision quest spoke about the Midewiwin scrolls and the Hopi prophecy. The Midewiwin, or Grand Medicine Society, is a secret curing society that endows members with supernatural powers. The scrolls teach the way of life that you are supposed to live; they teach the natural laws. The Iroquois have the Code of Handsome Lake. Before he became a prophet he was a raging alcoholic: it's all about purification. I'm helping others get sober now, in preparation. Then, if they do have an encounter, they will be reliable witnesses.

Standing for two days and two nights in my vision circle, the Little People said to me over and over again: "We're going to come back. We will talk again." In being sober and walking the Red Road and helping others to the road I am earning my next talk with the Little People. I won't go on the mountain again. Properly done, one vision quest is enough. Now I believe I am ready for the vision to seek me in daily life. These Little People I saw are going to come back and talk to me. And when I tell you about it, you will believe.

PRINCIPLES OF
RED ROAD RECOVERY

Look ahead   Toward the good Red Road   The great circle of life
Seated in the heart   Holding our closest affiliation   Human or
animal   Mother Earth or Father Sky   Recovery from addiction
Honor all the people   Walk the road with us   We do not walk
alone   Healing a deep and sorrowful spirit   Face the fear   Join the
flight   Wings of the great blue heron   Flying toward new beginnings
Joyful reunions   To traditions of the circle   Seeking honesty
through truth   In circles of meetings   Share the work   The inside
job   Practice the principles

The Sacred Hoop   Teaches our nature In four parts   Physical   Mental
Emotional   Spiritual   Develop balance   Health through volition
Doorway of the will We all must pass   Take the journey   Always
open   Pathway of infinite patience   Decide to travel   Actively
participate   Guides and teachers appear   Spiritual protectors   Watch
over the traveler

Four dimensions of the Sacred Hoop   Four cardinal points   Four
dimensions of being   Struggle to acquire new gifts: Timid become
brave   Weak become bold Insensitive become caring   Materialist
become spiritual

Community service   To keep the gifts   You must give them away
Uphold a life   Walking the good Red Road Into the prisons
Hospitals   Shelters   Schools   Rehab centers   Share the experience
Strength   Hope   Prayer and invocation   Gifts of the circle   Power
of the Sacred Hoop   The talking circle of all races   Healing a
spirit   Of all nations

3 WE WANDER THIS WORLD WITH A PURPOSE

Law of Light-Sound

MALI KEATING

> *The Hopi were survivors of another world that was destroyed. Therefore, Hopi were here first and made four migrations—North, South, East, and West—claiming all the land for the Great Spirit, as commanded by Massau, and for the True White Brother who will bring on Purification Day.*
>
> CHIEF DAN KATCHONGVA, SUN CLAN
> HOPI SOVEREIGN NATION

All through New England there are monolothic stone structures; the sites consist of underground chambers, standing stones, Sun altars, and earthen mounds. Many of these structures are astronomical alignments for solar equinoxes and solstices. Symbols drawn on rocks at these sites have revealed themselves as aspects of the original teachings. I was beginning to correlate these symbols with crop circles and sacred architecture, the mystery of which lies within the mathematics of the universe, a body of understanding known as sacred geometry.

Prior to departing for Roswell Mali Keating and I traveled to the Penobscot reserve at Indian Island, Maine. My friend and the very gifted carver, Stan Neptune, took us by canoe to another island, where we walked quite some distance into the woods. There he showed us an ancient site—a stone Sun altar, an underground chamber, and a mound. As the Sun went down the sundial pointed to the mound that the Sun was disappearing behind.

Following my interview with Mali I was inspired to render a drawing of the "mother crop circle" at Barbury Castle, England. The tetrahedron is a code aligning ancient structural sites from on and off this planet. Many of the crop circle formations are indigenous symbols found in the cultures of Mesoamerica.

Could it be that the language of sacred geometry speaks to the merging world of megolithic sites and crop circle formations? Both stand in harmony with the symbols of the universe, illuminating a gateway to the stars and the Master Teachers that traverse all dimensions. —NRS

Mali Keating is a sixty-eight-year-old elder and activist who has presided over innumerable Indian councils and organizations. Raised with grandparents from the Odanak reserve in Quebec, she is of the Bear Clan. Mother of four and grandmother of seven, Mali lives with her daughter and granddaughter in a turn-of-the-century farmhouse in Vermont. Continuing in her mother's illustrative footsteps, Mali's daughter is finishing a master of arts degree in Native American studies at Dartmouth College. Mali shared moose stew, squash, and most of an afternoon with me touching on a broad range of subjects near to both our hearts.

Almost every tribe has a legend that speaks about Sky People, about having come from the stars. The Hopi, specifically their Katsinas [Kachinas], are Star People. The Iroquois say that the first person was Woman-who-fell-from-the-Sky. My own adherence to tradition is Anishinabe, a tribe that originated on the East Coast. Because of Christianity we lost our traditions but the name of the tribal group survives, and the name itself means "man let down from the sky." In *The Mishomis Book* by Edward Benton Banai I found the literal translation: *ani* (from whence), *nisha* (lowered), *abe* (the male of the species).

Many artifacts that have been discovered over the centuries seem to indicate that there was an extremely advanced civilization here long before what we consider to be our recorded history. The Hopi are quite matter-of-fact about their connection with Star People existing here and now.

NASA recruited the help of Richard Hoagland, the curator of the Springfield Science Museum in Massachusetts, for the first flyby of Mars. Hoagland created an interstellar message communication system for the Pioneer 10/11 spacecraft. Over the years NASA used Hoagland's approach to record any communications that might be received during such flights.

☐ *Mali Keating*
Abenaki, Vermont

When I first met Richard Hoagland he was looking for elders who had knowledge of prophecies that might connect travel to Mars with American Indian oral traditions. One elder, an Apache woman, had told him of a tradition that talked about the Red Star, and which verified for him a connection between Mars and Indian people. In the years since the 1976 Viking mission, Richard Hoagland had been examining the pictures taken of the monuments on Mars. The pictures were taken at two separate times so the shadows were completely different, and yet the pictures revealed the same thing. On the edifice he saw a face, the appearance of which correlated with other ancient faces. It is very Sphinx-like in appearance. Using laser enhancement and other pictorial methods he was able to take measurements of what he considers to be a city that is very close to the face. In that city there's a large pyramid and an area that looks like a circular dome edifice. There looks to be a circle, like a moat, around it. Hoagland and his team of scientists took pictures of the dome and made a vinyl overlay, which they placed on a model of an ancient edifice in England. The structure, at Silbury Hill, is a similar rounded earthen dome with steps encircling it. There is a circular area around it and a pyramid close by. The overlay from the Mars photographs fits perfectly over the model of that ancient site in England. These two monuments are exactly the same; it is as if one is a reproduction of the other. What Hoagland found in the measurements time and again were tetrahedral metaphors, the same code found in Cydonian geometry and the sacred geometry of ancient temple sites, from Teotihuacán in Mexico to Giza in Egypt, from Stonehenge in England to Serpent Mound in Ohio. *[Tetrahedral geometry is part of a planetary physics that opens to other dimensions, the relationship of angles serving as a portal into the space/time continuum.]*

On February 27, 1992, on the eve of the return mission to Mars, Hoagland spoke at the United Nations. He presented all this information to the U.N. because he wanted them to know that people at NASA weren't listening to him. They had stopped giving Hoagland any information or allowing him to know anything about what they

■ *Palenque*
Ancient Temple Site, Paul Duarte

were doing. He was hoping the United Nations would pressure NASA into photographing this area again, to help come to some conclusion on it. "We have done every bit of research we can do with the existing pictures," he said. "With your help we can establish whether this is a fluke or a monument. If you make sure that the mission that goes up this time will go over that same area and take new pictures, then we can all examine this and verify it one way or the other." The U.N. ignored him.

When I met with Richard Hoagland in Washington, D.C. I was there to attend the investiture of Ada Deer as the assistant director of the Bureau of Indian Affairs. An organization that I chaired was one of the sponsors of the dinner. Richard Hoagland was doing a radio talk show. I had seen the U.N. briefing, and asked a mutual friend to arrange for us to meet. We were supposed to meet for lunch; we ended up spending the rest of the day and evening talking together. He asked me about the connection between Star People and the origins of Native Indian people. Hoagland had come to suspect that Mars had developed an advanced civilization that did to that planet what we are doing to Earth. He contends that an advanced civilization came *here* to escape the destruction of its atmosphere. Of course, Mars has no atmosphere left. But they have water that is frozen into the planet—a great deal of water. And what little atmosphere is left has taken the chemical composition that Earth's will take if we continue on the couse we're on. He was not only interested in substantiating this but in warning the scientific community that it is unleashing the same destruction. His interest is not only in finding out what happened on Mars but in using that information as a warning, because we are in no position yet to make the jump to another planet, like the Mars people may have.

Then in the fall of 1993 I met Thomas Benyaca, the speaker for the Hopi elders who fulfilled an ancient Hopi prophecy. This prophecy revealed that a Hopi elder would try for forty years to speak in a great house of mica in the East before finally being heard there. In December of 1992, the day after a total eclipse of the Moon, the greatest storm in New York's history tore at the streets and buildings while Thomas Benyaca sat at the U.N. waiting for his moment to speak. With hundreds of thousands of New Yorkers without power and the U.N. closing its ground floor, he took the podium to invoke the prophecy. When he was asked if the storm could be stopped he said yes, and formed a prayer circle. Perhaps you know that his name, Benyaca, means "water." The waters listened to the prayers he led that day. The storm ceased.

According to Hopi tradition there have been previous worlds—not separate worlds, but the same world with different civilizations on it. The First World was destroyed. The Second World came into being and eventually a certain people ruled. The prophecy didn't mean that the whole planet was destroyed; it meant that the civilization and way of life were changed.

Now the Hopi are talking about the coming destruction of Earth as we know it. This is something for which they are prepared, something they have been talking about for a long time. The Hopi are the oldest continuing civilization on this continent that we know of. The Mayans, the Aztecs, the Mound Builders—all those ancient people have ended. The Hopi continue. Their history goes back into the dim past, so far back that other people don't remember it.

■ *Aztechna Olmec Katsina (Space Traveler of Wind Energy)*
Marion Martinez, Kiowa

But that history is not a simple story, because even among the Hopi there are differing versions. One tradition says they came up from a different continent. The other says they came from a hole in the earth. The first tradition speaks of a high level of civilization on the missing continent, but this high civilization destroyed that world. This sect of the Hopi say that the Katsina People, the Star People, came and saved a portion of this civilization from catastrophe by setting them in metal cylinders in the water to ride out the destruction when the great continent sank. This story is about the continent of Atlantis. They told it to Frank Waters; it's in *The Book of the Hopi.* The elders felt that, since so many of the prophecies had been fulfilled, we were too near the destruction not to warn any who would listen.

Metal cylinders are what transported the survivors. Now, ceremonial kivas are round and they are set way down in the ground. According to some Hopi the kivas are shaped this way to represent those metal cylinders.

The second tradition, which speaks of the Hopi coming up from underground, seems to start at this point in the historical narrative. It begins with marooned survivors climbing out from under the wreckage of a holocaust. According to the first tradition, as the survivors climbed from the cylinders and set foot on island soil they could see other islands sinking in the sea behind them. They traveled north; when they finally reached the eastern coast of North America they were greeted by the great eagle, who gave a message to them that they were never to build cities.

The message indicated that before they could reach the ground that was set aside as their final place to live—though they were given tablets showing where this final place was—each clan would be given a different ceremony to fulfill. Each of these ceremonies was necessary to survival. If the Hopi didn't follow the ceremonies and the prayers they would destroy themselves. The instructions were to travel from the East Coast all the way north, to the frozen door of the north. Then to travel west, to the great ocean in the west. Then all the way south, to the great frozen door at the south.

They did that. The Hopi elders know all the great places they stopped, the monuments of their migration.

The Anasazi were a people left over from the migration. The people were told they must never stop and build cities, but of course some did. There would always be certain groups that would insist on stopping, not continuing on the migration. They would stop and make cities. Cities make people crazy, as we all know. People become greedy and lose the ability to work together.

Hopi elders who have visited the ruins of Aztec and Mayan civilization can read the inscriptions on the walls. One of the main points of the Hopi prophecy is that they know when this world ends. All Native people know of the cleansing, this great upheaval. The Hopi said that they would know that the end is coming when roads crisscrossed this continent like the web of a spider—those are the vapor trails of airplanes. You can see vapor trails like the webs of spiders in the sky.

When the United Nations came into being in the 1940s and it became known that a great building of glass was built, the Hopi said, "Ah, our prophecies say that the end is coming when a house of mica is built on the coast of the great eastern ocean. Here the heads of nations in the world will gather to debate. A Hopi elder must go there and bring the message to the heads of nations, and warn them that they are destroying Earth." The story goes like this. In the forties the Hopi chose four young men to be speakers for the elders. They would go to the U.N. and try to speak their message. The Hopi said they would knock on the doors of the U.N. four times. If they were not allowed to address the heads of nations then there would be nothing they could do to stop the cleansing, the Earth changes. It was agreed that four separate times they would bring this message to the U.N. The fourth and final attempt occurred with Thomas Benyaca in December of 1992.

In the Hopi prophecy the True White Brother, separated from the Hopi millennia ago, is to return with the other tablets. These are the important missing pieces to the puzzle of the survival of humankind. The True White Brother will return following the purification. We will only know who the True White Brother is when he returns carrying the tablets. The Tibetans hold tablets also, and have been in close contact with the Hopi.

I met Thomas Benyaca in New York City, when he and another elder came to the New York Law School in public forum. Afterward there was a question and answer period. One man asked, "What about crop circles?"

◘ *Eagle Man*
Michael Naranjo, Santa Clara Pueblo

The old, old Hopi man (with his son to translate, since the old man spoke no English) said, "Oh, yes, yes! We recognize the crop circles. Some of them are our symbols, sacred symbols off our petroglyphs. We have a photograph that was taken of a UFO on which these symbols appear. Would you like to see the photograph?" There was complete silence in the auditorium; the whole place went still. Everyone got more than they anticipated with that one. Then the man who asked the question said in this little bitty voice, "Yes." So they sent a young Indian man down to show him the photograph. You could have heard a pin drop while he was looking at it. There were no more questions after that.

Thomas Benyaca and I met at a coffee shop the next morning.

■ *The Mother Crop Circle*
Tula, Abenaki/Cherokee

He told me I was an elder of the Eastern Door. I told him of the Wabanaki Confederacy, elders from the Abenaki, Mi'kmaq, Penobscot, Maliset, and Passamaquady who serve as Keepers of the Eastern Door. Thomas said, "When the cleansing happens, your people must have this message—wait four years, four months, four weeks, four days, four hours, four minutes, and four seconds from today. Then your people must understand that the only way we can slow the cleansing and its terrible disasters is for the uniting of the Indian people to occur first." He said once that the four years and four months period is over, we have four years. That would bring us to 2002.

I said that I would bring that message to the east, and that is what I've been doing with the Wabanaki Confederacy. I have been working to mend the Sacred Hoop to the Eastern Door. The Hoop of the Indian Nations was broken in the east first, so it must be healed first here, for the good of all the Indian Nations. For the good of all the world.

LAWS OF LIGHT-SOUND

Visualize crop circles   Corn circles   Created by light-sound
Primeval spheres   Archetypal symbols   Ceremonial circles of the
galaxy   Ceremonial circles of the crops   Symbols of the cosmos
Geometric models   Luminous rings of corn

The prophecy of crop circles   Earth charts   Maps of the petroglyphs
Travel through time-space   Visit galactic gifts from   Sky Travelers
Ancient teachers   Honoring Mother Earth   Drawing medicine
wheels of the future   Under the guidance   Watchful eye of Star
Katsinas   Mandalas of maize   Electric-magnetic fields of corn

Envision earth mandalas   Circles within circles   Paths of initiation
Teaching cosmic orderly direction   Four directions   Natural divisions
of a circle   Four sacred directions   Elements of mathematical harmony
Traveling toward evolution   Circles Stalks are laid   Stalks are bent
Layers of circles   Energy patterns of light-sound

Meditate on laws of light-sound   On frequencies   Structure of the
cosmos   Waves of creation   Pulse of earth technology   Vibration
of light   A reflection of parallel worlds   Communicate with visitors
Enter the spiral of crop circles   Unity of all and one

Follow crop circles   Corn circles   Follow the road of creation

4 THE NEW ELDERS

Principles of Environmental Justice

FRED KENNEDY

*The recognized festivals of Thanksgiving
shall be the Midwinter Thanksgiving,
the Maple or Sugar-making Thanksgiving,
the Raspberry Thanksgiving,
the Strawberry Thanksgiving,
the Cornplanting Thanksgiving,
the Corn Hoeing Thanksgiving,
the Little Festival of Green Corn,
the Great Festival of Ripe Corn,
and the complete Thanksgiving
for the Harvest.*

GUYOWEEO
THE IROQUOIS GREAT LAW

A s I lay sleeping in the predawn light I was awakened by three figures standing at the foot of my bed. They were tall, at least six feet high. The outlines of their bodies cast a beautiful silhouette. Their hands were crossed, palms upon their chests. From their hands surged energy lights that filled my body. Their hands became lotus flowers.

I could not move. I could not speak. My body was vibrating. Without speaking they told me, "We are not going to Roswell. We will be at Hopi." Then they vanished. I could move again.

In that moment I knew there would be no Roswell '97 for me. My house was packed up, ready to go. I left then to become a runner.

The lavender light Fred Kennedy speaks of recalled the light emanated by the visitors I encountered. It was a healing light that carried language without words. At no time did I feel fear or even feel threatened. If being initiated includes being abducted, then this must be another course. The instructions being gathered are the seeds of our future harvest, if we plant them with our young.

The Little People and the Corn Pollen deities seemed familiar to me, encoded in distant memories. Fred speaks of the records of star heritage on story belts, and how we are waiting in prayer, doing work that needs to be done. —NRS

Fred Kennedy was born of the Beaver Clan on the Cattaragus reservation in upstate New York. Great Bear (Nugwite) is one of the last traditional carvers of the snow snake, a message-tipped spear thrown from village to village. Currently a champion thrower of the snow snake, headsman of his people, strawberry farmer, woodsman, father of three and grandfather of three, Fred maintains a traditional lifestyle, including living without running water.

■ *Fred Kennedy*
Seneca Nation, New York

In September or October of 1995 a craft was shot down at Montauk Point, Long Island, New York. I spoke to a man who was in the laboratory on Long Island when this happened. He'd actually seen the physical beings that were in the ship—he was on the removal team. We have the technology now to do this, to shoot these UFOs out of the sky using laser and plasma rays. Russia also has the same technology; they are more advanced than the average person knows.

Looking at our ceremonies on the ground you can see that everything is collected from the stars. For two thousand years the seven stars have been visible on the wampum belt. The seventh one is trying to break through now. It will come through the Milky Way; it will appear as a blue star.

The Creator handed us the wampum belt. It is the Great Law, our guideline for life. The Great Law is passed from one mouth to the other until the next generation comes along. Someone takes on a round that's been left out; they pick it up and it goes like this, like a snake. *[Fred puts his hands together to form the head of a snake and weaves them from one side to another.]* The teachings of the Great Law weave back and forth, but they stay on track.

Our wampum belt tells about how the Creator came across the great sea of sky. This is also described in the Mayan calendar, which lists the day the Sun sat on Earth but didn't burn it. When the star lands on Earth and doesn't burn, that is the creation. The Great Law says the day the Creator came over was the first time this continent heard thunder; it was the sound of the Creator paddling in the sky. It's all in the Great Law. The first star was the star of creation. The second star brought Woman-who-fell-from-the-Sky. With the third star animals appeared. The fourth star brought the prophet. With the fifth star came the people losing direction. The sixth star brings a new prophet who speaks all languages.

When that prophet is known to the world, we will be at the emergence of the seventh star. You see, now the story on the wampum belt

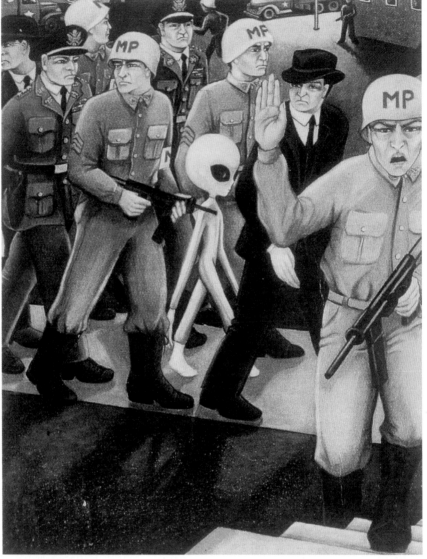

◙ *Roswell Crewman*
Lisa Busenberry

has reached its end. All its words have stopped. We are waiting now for the seventh star, the battle of the serpent, the battle of all the races. There are two sides to everything. And so we wait, too, for the new prophet from Turtle Island who will unite all the races in his struggle. The people of the shadow will destroy themselves in their greed.

Star Ancestors—we call them the Little People. Yes, when you add a spaceship ETs and Little People start to sound about the same. Little People have mysterious power. That's what I always heard from the old people when I was growing up.

Many say they've had encounters with the Little People. I have a story of a personal encounter to tell you. The night I broke my dog's back I was way up in Berne Springs. I went to hit a coon that was biting him and instead I hit my dog with a club. Now, I've worked in the woods my whole life. I struck to kill that coon, and I missed. I hit my dog across the back as hard as I could; he was crawling and whimpering in pain. His back was broken. He could hardly move. I was holding him and rubbing him when all of a sudden this light came, a lavender light that lit up the whole forest. After the light went away my dog shook himself, got up, and went off running again.

◘ *Little People*
Shona Bear Clark, Creek

He got the coon poisoning later. For that they usually have to put a dog down. I took my dog to the veterinarian and he said there was a hundred to one chance that my dog would not survive, but he would do what he could. My dog got coon paralysis; he lost all movement from his hips downward. The vet took one look at an X ray and yelled, "How the heck did your dog survive this?" That's when I realized he had a broken back. I knew it was the light that saved him, that transparent lavender light.

The Little People live and hold council in mounds. They dug some up on my Uncle Jack's land in Cattaraugus. They were in mummy form, only wrapped in red elm bark. They disappeared into a museum somewhere. The Little People lived here, but they knew how to beam out of here. They traveled. That's why their offspring are found in Peru. They are linked to the mound graves found in Peru.

You know the Hopewell Mound in Ohio? The rotted-out timber posts on the Ohio site were reconstructed; they provide a calendar more accurate than Stonehenge. They are like the Anasazi calendar towers of the Southwest, second only to the Mayan pyramids in terms of sophistication, on this continent anyway. Who taught this star knowledge over such distances? Was it traders, or wandering priests? Did a migratory sect of the Mayan culture travel with this knowledge? Did Star Ancestors seed this knowledge all over Earth?

Talking about the Little People is bugaboo for certain Indians, while for others it's sacred talk. You don't try to explain it to everybody because you feel that you're wasting your days. But actually our contact with the Little People is woven into our spiritual histories. You can't finish a story without mentioning them. Sacred talk is not supposed to fit together perfectly. It's not "prove it" talk. When you talk of the Little People respectfully, you're opening to them. Something clicks in your mind, and you go back into their lives with them. Then you see who they are. Some speak with us, some only show us their ways. But we connect with them.

I talk about the Little People because the time is so close! We talk now because we have to educate Earth people for when the Little People come back. Otherwise Earth people will go crazy and blow them up. These are some very high spiritual beings. From the prophecies I have heard, and from what I have experienced, they are returning within our lifetimes. The Little People are coming back.

Some elders have become so close-minded! Young people are talking about the Little People's return and the elders are trying to shut them up, saying, "We don't know nothing!" But they are not really the elders. The elders are the young people who are seeking the truth. Yes, it is the youth who are the true elders now. They are going to be learning from the times. They are going to take on tomorrow. We came from the time when you could sit back and relax. Now the kids know they better get in there and do it! Or they're not going to get anything. They're not going to be anything. They've got to go through it all: drugs, crime, every kind of temptation. The ones who survive are going to be the real people, new millennium children, the new elders, the Blue Ray babies. The young are different from the old. If a spaceship landed the young would say, "Oh man, that's so cool!" They would not be fearing it. An older person would say, "Run and grab your gun and shoot anything that comes out!" That's the difference between new and old. The old age involves guns, violence, alcohol, and wars. The children of the new age are involved with light, love, spaceships, and peace. That's why the elders get mad at me when I talk, because I say, "We're not the elders."

It was 1951 when they dug up those Little People at my uncle's land. There was big talk around here then. The secret talk came out and you heard about the Little People as being strong, so powerful. My old one-eyed uncle used to tell me that our people, the Seneca, chased the Little People into Ohio. That's how come the Seneca moved there. They were at war with the Little People.

At first they lived all around us in colonies, but we didn't communicate. We were afraid and stayed away from them. Then came a certain chief, a warrior, who said, "I'm going to show them just how great a warrior I am." He killed the son of one of the Little People. In retaliation the Little People stole the chief's baby. The Seneca sent a war party in chase which ended all the way in Ohio, where the Serpent Mound is. It is said that the Little People inhabit those mounds.

When the war party cornered the Little People in a mound the warriors couldn't penetrate the protective energy screen around it, so they camped around the outside and sent a single spokesman toward the mound. (The word for *force field* in the Seneca language translates as "not time to war, time to talk.") The warriors could not get past the field until they chose a messenger who carried no weapons. The spokesman was allowed into the mound. He was told that if the war party returned home, the son of the chief would be returned on the next Moon.

They did as they were instructed. The war party—turned peace party—arrived home shortly before the new Moon in May. Soon after, the baby was returned. It was the planting season. The Little People kept their promise; the Seneca ceased to be their enemies and became their friends. We sent people to Ohio to protect the Little People from the Shawnee. This is the old, old story of how we became connected to the Little People long before European contact.

It is said that the Little People could come and go off the planet. When they disappeared there was never talk about why. It was always said they had supernatural powers, which is why we stayed shy of them. The Little People understood all about the Moon and stars, which is where we came from. We were let down from the stars. The Little People traveled the galaxy. Our ceremonies, our seeds, our medicine, and our philosophy came from the Little People. All Indians talk about the Little People.

Look at the rock inscriptions on Kelly's Island at Lake Erie. There was a gathering there. Indians with headdresses showed up on an area off Sandusky. This is a sketch from the 1800s. Look at all the petroglyphs on the big rock. Archaeologists got mixed up at first trying to read it because the ice had turned the rock upside down, right at the edge of the lake. You look at the petroglyphs and you can see the watch-

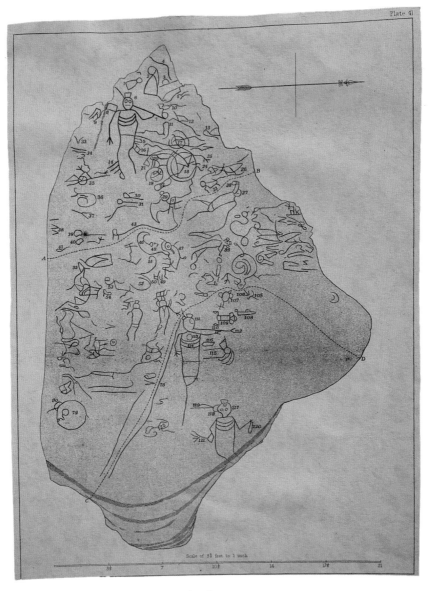

Plate 41

◾ *Rock Inscriptions on Kelly's Island*
From the journals of Captain S. Eastman, 1850

ers. You hear about the watchers for each coastline. They send you spirit in times when you really need it.

When I was there I saw the story of our Great Law on the rock. In the drawing you see the tall one, the being; he symbolizes travel.

These are conglomerates of people coming together in travel—the migrations. This is the meeting place. This is where it happened. These drawings are like hieroglyphs. They are formulas for any and all medicine—any and all travel—on and off this planet. All history and encounters with other beings from other realms are recorded in petroglyphs on rocks. The ancient symbols are codes of living, laws of survival. The big knowledge is in the inscriptions from the time travelers.

When Shepard orbited Earth in a Mercury spaceship in 1966, he picked up a beeping light from Earth. At first he thought it must have been from NASA, but it was coming from Serpent Mound in Adams County, Ohio, where they see ships all the time. The pulse of the equinox line takes off outside of Ohio; the strongest energy point anywhere across the United States is there. The Serpent Mound and all those underground pyramids are there. There is a no-flight zone over that area because airplane gauges go nuts there. The Serpent Mound was created as a monument to Haley's Comet; you can recognize the tail. But it was also a great center of teaching.

That area was called "Little Egypt" and then "Ohio." For the Shawnee the word *ohio* means "place of beginning." The Tibetan people also have a word *ohio*. For them it means the *dharma,* the teachings.

When we had the White Buffalo Ceremony elders came to Minnesota from all over the world. The White Buffalo prophecy belongs to the Lakota. The Inuit have their prophecy; the Cherokee, the Principal People, have theirs. They say when red flames dart across the sky in the pattern of a web that the purification is near. In the south, methane gas from all the coal burning turns red in the flight path of planes. So they have been seen, these flaming red webs in the sky, down in North Carolina. That is happening now.

Prophecy says that when all the races come together to understand

◨ *UFOpelli*
John Brower

each other the White Buffalo will turn white again. She almost turned to white this year, but it's not time yet. By next year maybe. The Red people have to come back together. No matter where we stand all eyes are on us now, for we carry the wisdom.

I'm still in the woods making medicine. I go on the north slope across the creek to look for moosewood and dogwood way up on the hillside. I get the medicine and bring it back for the people of the longhouse. There are big maple groves up there, and moosewood everywhere. The moosewood is good for drying congestion or phlegm, for drying up extra water in your system. Moosewood is strong medicine. There's a lot of good medicine out there, but most people don't believe in it anymore. They are hooked on an instant fix, on western medicine.

The mixture time is the most important fact of Indian medicine. You can't mix medicines out of season. You can only mix so much at one time, only what you need. The rest should be dried. A lot of people mix too much at once.

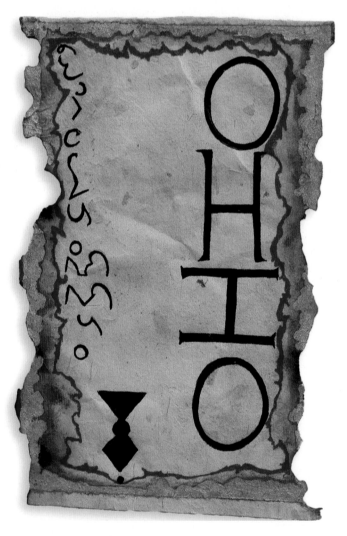

◼ *Tibetan Word For Ohio*
Tula, Abenaki/Cherokee

I make medicine with alder-tag, we call it "tac on the road." You have to dig for it way down in the swamp. Down on the bottom is a bush where the roots are, way down in the mud. The roots are like hairs. This is good liver medicine; it cures almost any liver problem. If you've got a really bad complexion, you wash those roots and boil them good, then chew them until they get soft. This medicine will take all the acne right out of your face.

You can take that alder-tag and peel it like cherry bark—just scrape the thin bark right off the top with a knife. You'll find little white bumps, and under those is green bark. Make a bundle with the green bark and drop that into boiling water, then turn the water off and let the bundle steep. Drink it twice, then make a new batch. This will purify your blood, taking all the impurities out.

Right now is the time to get the alder-tag, when the snow comes down. That's the time to start brewing medicine. Ninety percent of Indian medicines are brewed right now, in the wintertime. The strongest medicine, however, comes in the spring. That's sassafras. When the snow is melting in the spring you can take the buds off the branch. At this time the sassafras is very strong. Boil it if you want a treatment for rheumatism or gout. It's also good for fevers and systemic infections. If you want good air in your blood you go down to the stream and pick watercress. Eat this plant raw after washing it. This medicine is a good, strong blood oxygenator. It's good for the stomach too. When you eat watercress your mouth just fills up with water.

Barely anyone comes for medicine anymore. I know every bush, weed, and berry, and what their curative powers are. I'll go get anything for anybody, but people just aren't using it like they used to. The Creator gave us all the medicines we need. We have to take care of our Mother or we will lose it all.

The prophecy talks about people coming out of the sky to help us. That is what the talk has been from my grandmother, my grandfather, their grandparents, and back. My grandmother said, "People from the sky are going to help us and you'll see them!" But nothing will happen until we make it happen. We have to decide what we want. The Star People won't interfere. The Creator gave us free will and everything we need. We have all the beauty and natural surroundings. There is gold, there is oil, there is water, the Sun, the Moon, the stars, gas—everything we need is here, and we can enjoy everything but the by-product of our creations, which is pollution.

Look at that bird feeder out there. I can see the whole world in that bird feeder because the birds don't come anymore. How long does the season last? How brilliant is the fall? All these mark the tides of pollution. The birds don't come like they used to and some don't fly like they used to. Their lungs are shot from pollution. They have to live with the pesticides and drink contaminated water. The animals have no place to go to hide from pollution. They are the most exposed, and we are losing the animals, one by one.

So we do our Rabbit Dance, our Snake Dance, our Smoke Dance. We use our rattles and mark the time and the seasons of our footpath. And I wait for the time when the people from the sky return to help us.

PRINCIPLES OF
ENVIRONMENTAL JUSTICE

The new elders The watchers Children's eternal fire Honoring
mind Heart Spirit Voices In the wilderness The fire keepers
Warming Children's eternal life A drum circle A blanket dance
A round dance Disarming for peace

Environmental justice For generations to come Mother Earth
Father Sun Sister Moon Oneness Cyclical spiritual flow Children
of all nations Protect Mother Earth All her life Will balance the
world

Toxins Hazardous waste Radioactive material Poisons Nuclear
testing Contaminant storage Extraction Production disposal
Plutonium Chemical warfare Chemical choices

Are we honoring our youth? Honoring our future? Global sisterhood
Global brotherhood The new elders The watchers Watching us

Mother Earth has been consumed How will she replenish? As the
veins of her rivers swell Turning inside out Collapse and disappear Has
she been honored? As she cracks Dry and brittle An unquenchable
thirst Sucking life's juices From her womb Oils and minerals Metals
and ores Elements of nature

Earth changes will restore her Washing inside out Mother Earth is
purification Calling a cleansing For all beings

5 THE STAR NATIONS ARE HERE TO HELP US

Healing the Four Races

TROY LANG

The Ancient Astronauts

I come from the Red Star
by way of the Red Lightning
on the path of the Red Rainbow.
I am the Beautiful Seven.

RAVEN HAIL, CHEROKEE

The prophecies speak of ancient scientists from the sky rescuing Indian people from a sinking Atlantis and instructing them to make their migration. Mainstream America calls these scientists *extraterrestrials.* Indians call them Star Beings, Sky Guardians, Star Ancestors, or simply "deities."

The destruction of Atlantis and the subsequent migrations through Mesoamerica lie within the mystery of Indian knowledge of our ancestors from the sky. The Star Beings showed us where we came from. They taught us how to read the stars, how to build pyramidal ceremonial centers, how to keep a cosmic calendar. They taught us how to honor our place of origin from the stars, how to reconnect with it and with those who seeded us here. The migration stories contradict conventional anthropology, which claims Indians came from Asia, across the Bering Strait into Alaska, and down into America. Some Indians contend that it was the other way around—the migrations came through Mesoamerica after the sinking of Atlantis.

For months I had been interviewing elders in the United States about UFOs, ETs, and sky deities. The vision seemed dark, the winter was cold. I was told to make the pilgrimage to the Yucatan, to the temples of cosmic knowledge. "The farther you go for medicine, the stronger it is": that is what is said of this stone lodge.

I have completed five interviews now. The pieces of the puzzle are fitting together. The center of the circle is in the Yucatan, so I must make that trip for the spring equinox. I will go to the Temple of the Seven Powers, Dzibilchaltún, to see dawn illuminate the portal of this cosmic watchtower.

I seek the citadels of light to illuminate my path toward knowledge for the higher purpose of the Greater Good. —NRS

Troy Lang was born of the Red Paint Clan in Asheville, North Carolina. His mother was a full-blooded Cherokee, his father a Berber from North Africa. His indigenous name, Rolling Thunder, foretells the deep voice with which he speaks and sings. Troy's love of music and his commitment to activism—as a charter member of the International Treaty Council, which holds a seat at the United Nations—force him to live in a high-rise apartment in New York City, a place his Indian mind abhors. Here, in a small living room packed with videotapes documenting every statement he will make, we talk of Star Ancestors.

M y grandmother was from the Red Paint Clan. She was known to dream, and was able to interpret dreams. The dream world is a parallel world; she walked between the two worlds.

I experienced incidents that I wasn't afraid of until I got older, when I reflected on my childhood. For example, one morning my grandmother said, "I don't want you to ride the bike today. I want you to stay home." So I said okay, and as soon as the house was empty and my chores completed I went to see my favorite great aunt, who lived across town. I got on the bicycle and proceeded to her house. About five blocks from my aunt's house a car hit me. The entire front wheel of the bike was demolished, but I did not even get scratched. The guy who hit me was so happy I wasn't hurt that he took the bike to a shop and had the whole front end replaced.

After the bike was fixed I went on to my aunt's house. I never told anyone I got hit by a car. The next morning my grandmother said, "You know, I had a dream last night that you got hit by a car, so I don't want you to ride the bike today." I did not tell my grandmother about the incident for ten years.

■ *Troy Lang*
Cherokee Nation, North Carolina

When anybody in the family was sick my grandmother would heal them. She had the herbs and the curative powers. I remember one time in the summer—I was four or five years old—my aunt had gone to the icebox to cut us some watermelon. Suddenly there was a lady standing in the hallway. My grandmother and my great aunt started crying. Nothing was said.

About seven years later we were all sitting around the table. I don't know what made me do this, but I said to my great aunt, "When I was little we were going to the icebox one summer day to get some watermelon. You started crying and there was a woman in the house." I asked, "Who was that woman? I never saw her before." Everybody at the table stopped; there was silence. My grandmother and my aunt looked at me, then they began to talk. My great aunt's sister had died and her spirit visited the house. When my great aunt saw her spirit, she cried. From that day on my family expected the visit of her spirit.

I know that Indian people are special people. I also believe that we

◼ *Sitting Bull*
Marcus Amerman, Choctaw

came from someplace else. As a kid I used to have a psychologist to talk to at school. He would counsel the Indian children because we grew up so differently. The way my grandparents and parents talked and lived was the Indian way. They took us out at night to look up in the sky and would say, "The sky is our camping ground in the stars. That is where we went, and that's where we came from." It was always taught that we came from the stars. Yes, our ancestry is of the stars. All Indians will say the same.

In my house the Sun never rose while my parents were in bed. They got up every morning before the Sun rose to do their prayers. The Navajo call this the Blessing Way. The Cherokee call it Keepers of the Eastern Door. That is the ritual that goes with the responsibility for keeping the prayers and ceremonies for the Eastern Door, where the Sun rises. Before dawn is when the gifts are bestowed. In the teachings I learned as a child there was always a relationship to the stars and to the Star People. When I was growing up I did not pay much attention. Within the last ten or fifteen years I remember those teachings.

I believe the Star Ancestors are already here. My relatives didn't use the words *extraterrestrial* or *space travel*. They spoke of the Little People. In our language we say *tsunsti,* "ancient astronauts." We know what is happening in the skies. At one time we lived in Dayton, Ohio. People of all colors in that part of the world know that UFOs are a reality. We used to set out lawn chairs at my house on summer nights and stare off toward the air base. We saw colored lights like you've never seen on Earth, moving faster and shining with an intensity that defies description.

We Cherokee are the people of the Red Star, the Morning Star, Venus. We are *aniyunwiya,* real human beings. We are the Red Star people, the Principal People, descendants of the great Mound Builders. Our ancestors built the "Little Egypt" of the Ohio Valley, Indiana, Illinois. Our relatives were of the technologically advanced Hopewell culture—the Cahokia people, the Adena, the Aztalan, and others. Our origin was in Mesoamerica. We migrated north to become the Mound

Builders of the Ohio Valley. There we built huge burial and effigy mounds—the powerful Serpent Mound in Adams County, Ohio, is the largest serpent effigy mound known to man. We too practiced cranial deformation, like the Mayan people.

[At this time Troy instructed me as an elder brother.] I feel that you have a calling. This is your walkabout, your vision quest. These are your instructions. Look into the past and you will see your future. The trail of evidence is still here, the structures are still here. We can see them. We can touch them.

The Bering Strait theory of Indian migration is ass backwards. The migration from Atlantis went through Mesoamerica into the four directions. At one time we all sat in a circle in Mexico. We had the technology in Atlantis of a very advanced civilization. The records have been destroyed; however, we had an advanced technology and we misused it. That is why this time around Indian people are a land-based spiritual people—at this time we do not have the ships that go on the water, above the water, and under the water, as in Atlantis. We got this technology from our Star Ancestors.

Due to their geometric proportions the sacred structures of Mesoamerica are connected with the magnetized forces of Earth. At these great pyramids Mayan priests sent messages to any place on Earth. The pyramids of Mesoamerica are related to the Cahokian ceremonial centers, as well as other ancient structures of North America. Some of these cities still function as they did before Columbus. One example is Tiahuanaco, part of the Andes culture, where they practiced raised-field agriculture. Scientists recently studied the patterns of these fields. They created a computer overlay of the fields from which they deduced that the field patterns related to the position of the Sun, and specifically to heat storage. The raised fields were restored to their natural ways. Scientists unearthed the entire water system to restore the irrigation and then planted crops. During the day the Sun heated the water; the water became so warm you could bathe in it. The system retained heat so that at night, when the Sun dropped, the stored

◧ *Cakohia (Hands)*
Marcus Amerman, Choctaw

heat built a cloud over the field, protecting the crops from frost.

I know we received advanced technology from high beings, from other galaxies. We destroyed the Third World with abuse of technology on Atlantis. We were rescued by the Star Nations, the Creator; the survivors landed in Mesoamerica, the birthplace of the last migration. That was the center, and from there we traveled the four directions—north, south, east, and west—building pyramidal monuments in each sector. In Tibet the great white pyramid was built in the Himalayan mountain range; in Cambodia, the pyramid of Angkor; in Egypt, the pyramid on the Giza plateau.

Go to the Yucatan for the spring equinox. Stand at the Temple of the Seven Powers and witness the dawn through the cosmic portal. You will see the full flourishing of our ancient culture there.

Scientists recently studied the DNA of Ramses II. He had some fifty wives and many children. His DNA and that of other royal mummies had traces of cocoa leaves and tobacco. Cocoa leaves come from

Central America. We are related to each other and to a great civilization from the stars.

Last night I was invited to the Museum of Natural History. I was asked to meet a delegation of Siberian Indians. They had come to New York City to bring their drum, their songs, their dances. They gave their drum to the Museum of Natural History. They brought the drum to the Eastern Door, the door of the Dawn Land.

We have the medicine. We have always had the medicine, the medicine of the seeds. Our drum is the heartbeat of our people. We save our medicine in our songs, in our dances, in our ceremonies. We are fulfilling the prophecy of our forebears as the custodians of Mother Earth. The prophecy is held within our circles and is unfolding for the worlds on Mother Earth. Earth changes have got to come, but we have some good seeds here, my sister.

I believe the ancestors are already here. They see what is going on. The new millennium is marking the time for the changing of the guard. The White race can choose two paths—the Black Road of Destruction or the Red Road of Spirit. The sacred circle cannot be complete as long as one of the race colors thinks it is the boss of all the colors. We cannot have balance and harmony unless we recognize each other as equal. We are all related. The White man, the Red man, the Yellow man, the Black man: the four colors. I've always admired my Asian brothers and sisters, particularly the Buddhists. They feel the same way about the truths that we Indian people have been trying to speak to the White men ever since contact. Now we all see the prophecy coming to pass. Chief Seattle spoke about how the land is not ours, and the animals are not ours. We are the custodians. If you are going to take this responsibility from us, then you have to assume it.

The White man has not assumed this responsibility, following instead the path of greed and power with technology. Now we're faced with el Niño, a weather pattern born of pollution from fossil fuels and chemicals, from a world out of balance. We see climate changes, strange seasons, big storms. In some places we have droughts, in some places

◘ *Spirit of the Drum*
  Shona Bear Clark, Creek

we have floods, in some places earthquakes. The cycles of nature are out of balance. We have a mild winter, then it is gone. We move right into spring, quickly again, and then summer. There is no long planting season, and the seeds in the east are wasted by flooding or saturated by too much rain. In some places there is so little water that seeds don't take or bear fruit. So altogether we have a shorter growing season. Now we have the threat of germ warfare. The Hopi call this time "the World Out of Balance." So it is.

Yes, we are standing at the crossroads. The Earth changes are happening now. Mother Earth is turning inside out, throwing off the toxins. The human races have to regain their humanity to survive. The whole planet will receive a healing. The change has got to come.

We Indians have stayed on the course, we have not strayed from the Great Spirit. We are a product of our ancestors. We have taken the responsibility for seven unborn generations to carry the guardianship. It's in our DNA, and the Great Mystery of it is in the good medicine. We don't sell the medicine, just like we don't sell the land. It's not for sale. As the poet and singer John Trudell says, "We are going to starve the Monster Technology so the Earth can breathe."

My only fear is that I will die before I fulfill my work helping to heal the races. Dying is not the end, however. It is the beginning of the new. Just as with the prophecy—it is the end of the old, the beginning of the new. The changing of the guard marks the new millennium. We've got the good seeds here, sister. Now is the time to go home and plant them.

The prophecy of the Principal People is generosity—to share the teachings with all peoples. Our tablets say we, the Cherokee, came here from the Pleiades. What was given is to be given now to all humans. We say *wado*—thank you—to all the ancient ones who have protected and kept these teachings for our generation to share. We have come full circle. So let us remember, we are of one race—the Humans—living the principle of appreciation for each other and our universe of all living beings.

HEALING THE FOUR RACES

Teachings From a crop circle Five concentric circles Orbit paths Around a Sun Circles of life Five circles of beings Four races of humanity White nation Black nation Yellow nation Red nation

Five concentric circles Orbit paths Around a sun The first orbit Near the nucleus Is the White race Responsible for fire Caretaker of fire The nuclear bomb is fire The White race has forgotten The responsibility of fire

Five concentric circles Orbit paths Around a sun The second orbit Is the Black nation Responsible for water Caretaker of water The waters are contaminated The Black race has forgotten The responsibility of water

Five concentric circles Orbit paths Around a sun The third orbit Is the Yellow nation Responsible for air Caretaker of air The air is polluted The Yellow race has forgotten The responsibility of air

Five concentric circles Orbit paths Around a sun The fourth orbit Is the Red man Responsible for earth Caretaker for earth The earth is dying The Red race is losing The responsibility for earth

Five concentric circles Orbit paths Around a sun The fifth orbit Is the Star nations The Star nations are here to help us The Earth is out of balance

Together the five nations Are entering a new cycle The prophecy of all races Balancing the elliptical orbit

6 ET IS HERE

Rituals for Visitation

OSCAR RODRIGUEZ

We go to return to our mansion, to rest in our community, for our time here has come to an end and it is the hour of departure. For that reason comes our all powerful lord: the comet, furrowing the sky with great power and glory, marking the time of the end of our era. We have come here only as pilgrim visitors. Already our mission is completed. Our days have terminated! Neither forget us nor think that we will not return! We are always in your memory, and you will think of us continually.

POPOL VUH (SACRED BOOK)
VERSE 778

Iattended the equinox ceremony at Temple of the Dzibilchaltún—the Shrine of the Seven Dolls, which, on the day of the equinox, is referred to as the Temple of the Seven Powers. I arrived in the predawn darkness with clusters of Mayan pilgrims from near and far—men in their pancho blankets, women in ceremonial white. In the dim, gray light I noticed a couple of westerners in the crowd, but no tour buses. Cars were parked along the rough roads at the jungle's edge. We walked in hushed anticipation, weaving along the footpath.

Entering the ruins of the city, the scrub undergrowth opened into a long, majestic promenade, bordered on either side with stone walls half-overgrown with jungle. Coming to rest at the approximate center of a four-directional cross, I focused my eyes on the huge stone temple rearing up in the darkness before me. A pale light, unencumbered by clouds, shimmered all around the twin legs of stone, announcing the nearness of dawn.

Taking a tobacco blessing from my bag and placing it before me at the Eastern Door, I blessed the four directions of my journey in the footsteps of the ancient four migrations. Intellectually, I suspected I was near a place of emergence.

All around me people were claiming their seats on the ground, forming their circles, the place from which each would behold the dawn, get the medicine, worship the Earth star. As the glow on the horizon threatened to spill its first light I hurried off the main promenade, hastening to a quiet spot a few feet from the jungle groves.

A glowing orange sky reddened, and the sun's molten edge crept into the bottom of the great stone window.

The light spread firelike up the masonry. To either side of this rectangular portal two smaller circular windows likewise flooded with orange crimson flame. The mathematics of the architecture! The sureness with which it celebrated the dawn light! The science overwhelmed me, as much as the astounding physical beauty of the Creator's eye staring me down. This is the technology of the Star Ancestors on Earth.

In front of me a group of white-clad Mayans, immersed in a trance state, silently raised their arms before them and then on up over their heads, spreading the fingers of both hands wide to the skies and waving their limbs through a flowing river of red light. The fire-flooder floated higher up the chimneylike altar atop the temple, disappearing from its brief enthronement.

The outline of the temple softened as this Mother Star's rays sputtered into the gold we call daylight. As the Sun emerged at the top of the chimney, dawn was over.—NRS

◻ *Dzibilchaltún, Temple of the Seven Powers*
Paul Duarte

▣ *Oscar Rodriguez*
Tarahumara, Quintana Roo, Mexico

◈

Oscar Rodriguez was born in Mexico City in 1943. He first saw pictures of flying saucers in American magazines, which he could not read. His mother was Tarahumara Indian from Chihuahua, his father Castillian Spanish. At age fourteen Oscar came to the attention of Diego Rivera, who took him on as a protégé and inducted young Rodriguez into the muralist painting union. Researching UFO books, Oscar learned some English. As an artist and cultural historian whose work is held in museums and private collections around the world, Rodriguez embodies the aesthetic conscience of the Yucatan, where he believes extraterrestrials appear now as they did thousands of years ago. A dynamo of energy at age fifty-six, Oscar was difficult to reach. He is the father of one son, grandfather of two, and great-grandfather of two.

H*ola,* and yes, we shall speak now. The extraterrestrials are announcing themselves to certain people—but the journey I had to take before I could say this to you! So, you must hear!

In 1993 the pope came to the Yucatan to talk to the Maya. I was chosen to create a present for the pope. I thought a lot about what to give him. A painting? A sculpture? I found an idea within the Popul Vuh, the Mayan Bible and the book of Mayan genesis, which is the genesis of America. The day I was to present my design to the church officials I changed my mind. I shouldn't create from the Popol Vuh, I realized. The gift for the pope was the cross, the Cross of Palenque! Among the most famous of ruined temples, Palenque is the sanctuary with the tomb of the great high priest Pacal Votan. He broke the Age of Blood, ending the sacrifices and ushering in the "Era of Light."

So I went to my meeting with the president of Mexico and the high

◼ *Cross of Palenque*
  Oscar Rodriguez, Tarahumara

church officials. I told them the Cross of Palenque was the only pre-Hispanic symbol that is in total agreement with the Occidental cross. Here it is; I wear a small reproduction around my neck. *[At this point Oscar removed the cross and showed me its inscriptions, and its symbols: the arrow with the feather, crossed by the snake's skin.]* The Cross of

Palenque, in fact, is a pre-Mayan symbol for the growth of mankind—the symbol for human evolution. It is not about the crucifixion; it is the prophecy of the great crossroads we now face.

The council for the pope accepted the project. I was given a permit and I started doing numbers. It was a very expensive project. Finally I received the funding. I created many designs, small crosses of all shapes and sizes. Five final designs were given to the president, the administration, and the banks.

After the decision on design was made I sent for the finest jade and gems from China for the central stone of the cross. We had just opened relations with the Vatican in Rome, and many banks were involved. I worked against time—twenty-one days, with my wife and crew assisting me. By then the strange happenings surrounding this project inspired me to make a film of the experience. Without resting we started filming, and even found time to go back and re-create what hadn't been filmed.

The 12th of August was the gorgeous day we arrived at Ak'e. There were jubilant stars in the sky that night. We set up our equipment at two o'clock in the morning to shoot the secret audience with the pope at four o'clock. For me the occasion was fantastic! The cross was given to the pope, and this magnificent ordeal was complete, but I'd not slept for a week.

Our schedule demanded that we go immediately to Palenque, where troubles began to plague us. First, the monkeys at Palenque went absolutely crazy, terrorizing my wife, myself, and the crew. The monkeys are the guardians of the temple, you know. No one had ever seen them like that, not even the federales.

We had permits from the Institute of Archaeology in Mexico City to shoot footage at night. So we had no choice but to sleep there, at the Temple of Inscriptions, near the great jade sarcophagus of the Master Sorcerer. It was from this tomb that the great Cross of Palenque was stolen years ago and thrown into the nearest river. It was recovered and restored, only to be locked up in the Museum of Anthropology in Mexico City.

The tomb looks like a woman's uterus. A channel comes from the top of the tomb; this was the channel for the fresh blood of the virgins. Pacal Votan opposed this ritual.

The body of Pacal is different from the body of other Mayan people—you can tell this from the size of the tomb. It is much larger than most. Some say Pacal Votan was a direct descendent of the Star People.

I brought all my lights down into the tomb but every light I turned on blew out, and all the expensive cameras broke. I ended up using my handheld camera with a built-in light attachment.

Despite the angry monkeys I have footage that is from another world, another dimension. The footage from Palenque came back from the lab with strange markings all over it—spheres looking as though they were coming from the distance. I could see the perspective in different cuts of the footage—I could visually determine that they were coming from far away. Inside of the spheres there were lights.

At first I thought these markings were water drops; however, they appeared in many parts of the film from that night at Palenque. I called the lab and asked them to examine the master. The lab announced that the spherical shapes were not water stains or any other damage; they were part of the photographic images taken at the temple.

Shortly thereafter I was telephoned by a rogue anthropologist friend who travels through the Yucatan uncovering hidden sanctuaries. My friend remembered similar incidents described in a book called *The Mayan Factor.* The next day I bought the book; sure enough, it described spheres obscuring the photographs of certain relics in the book. The spheres are called "artifacts," and are said to have been left by ancient astronauts.

In our conversation the anthropologist described a village where a spacecraft appeared. A creature came from the craft and then fell dead. The villagers covered the ship. They put the extraterrestrial being into a metal box because it was cool inside. They showed the creature to my friend, and allowed photographs and measurements to be taken.

▣ *Cosmic Astronaut*
   Kim Garcia, Lacondon

Later I saw one of the photographs—it was a very strange picture. The being in the photograph looked old, with large eyes. It was a very strong photograph. The creature measured 19 centimeters long, but its head was 14 centimeters long. Indeed, it was a very strange being.

When my friend visited this village he was with another man, an expert in computers. They tried to take exact measurements of the being by computer. They started using a scanner and the computer broke. They tried to scan the photograph into another computer and it too broke. Finally the technician took the photo to the most powerful computer he had access to. They scanned it successfully. Then, when the face appeared on the monitor screen, its eyes opened. It was alive. Was it a hologram? Some special message? I don't know. But I am now applying for permits to go back and film the village.

I am a Mayan historian and collector of pre-Hispanic artifacts. I am an historian of the peoples of the Yucatan. There are ancient histories of war between the Maya and supernatural beings. One story is in the Ramayana, a Hindu book, certainly one of the oldest. The Maya had technologies that could only be appreciated as magic. The cosmic mathematics that levitated stones and built the pyramids defy time; in fact, they disprove time altogether. There are stories of ancient Maya who live underground today. They are tall and fair-skinned. They are ambassadors for the extraterrestrials.

It is my belief that the Maya are Atlanteans, from the continent of Atlantis. I believe there are strong connections between the Maya, the Tibetans, and the Indians of North America. The culture the Atlanteans gave to us is the knowledge they had of the universe, the prophecy of the future worlds. They gave us books—books inscribed on rocks—and monuments—the pyramids of Egypt and the Yucatan, Stonehenge, the Serpent Mound. They gave us sacred geometry. And they have given us a choice to preserve humankind, but we don't seem to learn.

◙ *Pacal and Serpent*
Marcus Amerman, Choctaw

Maybe now, approaching destruction, they will return to help us build. They are going to appear, to instruct us on how to survive. We will be taught how to survive with a totally different mind-set as we become universal man. The greater way is to share. We have not learned that yet. Sharing is the answer. Maybe what life is about is to share everything.

I believe the Star Ancestors are already here. There are remnants of the Maya living underground in caverns and caves along the ocean. In the caverns and caves there is fresh water. The villagers bring them food and do ceremonies with them at night. I am going to try to speak with them, to give their message to the world. You will come with me, no?

RITUALS FOR VISITATION

Rituals in temples   Ancient time portals   Wellsprings of knowledge
Request through meditation   To understand the cycle   The ancient
calendar   Unraveling the truths

Rituals of our Sun   Symbol of a circle   Symbol of a square   Ceremony
for sacred geometry   Micro and macro   Paths of knowledge   Practice
the steps   Alone   And in unity

Between the Sun and Moon   See the great woman   Watching   The
cycles of time   Magnetic liberation   A sitting posture   Practice
meditation   Gifts of mental discipline   Freeing to enter   The light

Invocation of mantras   Love songs   For Mother Earth   Ask for her
teachings   Through ritual   Learn how to live   Visit the pyramids   Visit
the earth mounds   Visit the stone temples   Sanctuaries of stars

Rituals for visitation   Light shrines   Activating the seven powers   The
serpent kundalini   Forces of spirits Inhabiting temples of light   Earth
power zones   For time travelers   Beings that live   Inside and
outside   Our dimension

In your life   Four symbolic races   Part of the family   Brothers and
sisters   Living on Mother Earth   Four elements   Powerful and
distinctive   Part of the physical world   Respected equally

7

THE FARTHER YOU GO FOR THE MEDICINE, THE STRONGER IT IS

Solar Initiation of Mystery Schools

HUNBATZ MEN

> When the iron eagle flies and horses run on
>   wheels,
> the Tibetan people will be scattered over the Earth
> and the dharma will go onto the land of the Red
>   Man.
>
> TIBETAN PROPHECY
>
> When the iron bird flies, the red-robed people of
>   the East
> who have lost their land will appear, and the two
>   brothers from across the great ocean will be
>   reunited.
>
> HOPI PROPHECY

At the spring equinox ceremony at the Temple of the Seven Powers, in the moment that dawn became daybreak, a prismlike spectrum burst over the ground. Everyone and everything was transformed into hundreds of pyramids of colored light—kaleidoscopic honeycombs—a prismatic field supersaturating everything. I knew this pyramid prism; it held the colors of the chakras, the healing colors of matter, of energy. The portal of stone that is the temple represented a technology based upon ancient laws. *This* was the science of the Star Ancestors. What in the East is called the kundalini—the serpent yoga—is the Snake Dance for the Hopi. But instead of this consciousness rising up the spine, on that equinox dawn the benediction came from the Sun itself.

Now here I am, a few hours later, at Ak'e. As the *cambuta,* the conch-shell horn, sounds, Hunbatz Men leads a human procession up the steps of this ceremonial center. Moving between the monolithic pillars we form a pattern of the snake, to merge with the planetary serpent found in the equinox sky this day. Into these ceremonial centers the true teachers have brought the tempest of whirlpools of change, announced by the great suns that govern us. The cosmic/human alignment today marks the cycle of the new Age of Light. Through temple rituals I remember how to express my love of Mother Earth within the cosmic dance. She is in great danger through modern society's mishandling of natural resources. I have requested through prayer that she teach me how to better live with her so that we can have thousands more years of life on this Blue Star.

These rituals can be carried to any corner of Mother Earth to activate sacred sites. During the ceremony I learn how to begin reconnecting the seven powers of my physical body with the spiritual forces at the temples. In this way I reawaken the great power within—the "eye" of the godhead encoded with the memories of all peoples in all times. In the new time of light I will be better able to serve human beings and other beings that live outside of this third dimension.

My initiation will continue as I gather the knowledge placed before me. I must choose the seeds that will bring spiritual nourishment. —NRS

Hunbatz Men is a Mayan elder, Day Keeper, and caretaker of the ancient wisdom. For untold generations his family has been the protector of Mayan traditions, teaching only a select few. Chosen at age one, Hunbatz began his studies with his uncle, Don Beto. Today at fifty-five, with five decades of knowledge behind him, Hunbatz has chosen to "open up" the teachings of the Mayan calendar. As with other keepers of the secret societies around the world, Hunbatz Men has ruled that the old taboos no longer apply. Combining generosity with urgency, he shares the secrets of the spiritual science of the cosmos. Author of several books and lecturer of vast experience, Hunbatz Men emanates masculinity, kindness, and a most gentle wisdom.

M*a-lo-keem* (greetings) my sister. I am pleased for your visit. At 10 a.m. on this day, March 21, 1998, the planets Mercury, Saturn, and Mars will form the head of the Cosmic Serpent of Wisdom. The Sun and Moon, as well as planets Jupiter and Venus, will form the rest of his body, which will glide along from east to west, toward the Pleiades. The Serpent of Wisdom will be traveling toward the Pleiades to combine all of its planetary powers with the great power of the Pleiades, "the tail of the serpent."

◼ *Hunbatz Men*
Maya, Yucatan, Mexico

The planetary bodies in our solar system will travel for their rendezvous with the great Serpent of Wisdom. The Cosmic Serpent marks the calendar cycle; the cosmic flight marks the cycles of time. On March 21, 1997, we were sent the great messenger called Comet Hale-Bopp. This comet emerged near the Sagittarius region, where the Ophiuchus-Serpens constellation is located. The messenger came to tell us about great cosmic changes. Call it comet or planet, Hale-Bopp brought a great cosmic message of change; from now on all bodies, including that of the human being, will have their powers aligned for the initiation, the awakening. That was the message of Hale-Bopp.

Among the Mayan cosmic calendars there is one with a cycle of 26,000 years, which is divided into four equal parts of 6,500 years. Since the orbital cycle of Hale-Bopp is 3,250 years, or half the time period of 6,500 years, then with the presence in 1997 of Hale-Bopp we entered into the new calendar cycle of the Great Cosmic Change. With the alignment in the sky today we connect with the planetary bodies: the seven planets, the seven chakras, the seven powers. We are taking into our bodies the sacred planetary proportion. We use this sacred proportion to project ourselves to the Pleiades and to awaken our seven powers, which are connected to the seven great stars of this cluster.

We Maya believe we are cosmic humans. Each of us has our planetary identification. Our ancestors are from some place in the cosmos; our ancestors are of the cosmic family. All of our knowledge and power is born from the heavenly cycles. As the planets have different colors, so do we have different race colors. With the planets you have one that is more red, one more black, one more yellow, and one more white. You see, we cosmic humans have a similar identification. The man has more identification with the Sun, the woman has more identification with the Moon. To regulate the woman you have the Moon. To regulate the man you have the Sun. Some planets affect us in the day, some at night. So we look similar, but exist differently. We are each of us aligned with some planet. Mother Earth, for the Maya, she has other sisters out

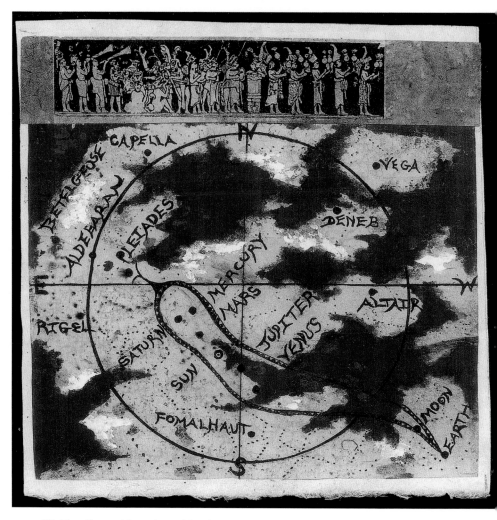

◧ *The Sky at Noontime,* March 12, 1998
Tula, Abenaki/Cherokee and Kin Garcia, Lacondon

there. That is one of the reasons we are connected to the Seven Sisters, the Pleiades.

A long time ago our ancestors of Maya did rituals to the planets, and our ancestors who traveled to Earth educated the Maya people. *[Hunbatz gestured to my illustration of the sky at noontime, March 21, 1998.]* With this map and with ritual we travel back to the Pleiades, our Seven Sisters of origination. For today is the spring equinox, and the magnetic alignment. These ceremonial sites on Mother Earth are where our ancestors settled to learn from her and to pay homage. Look at other pyramidal sites within the United States and their ancient connection with the timeless Maya. Look at Cahokia ceremonial centers in the United States. Earth is suffering now because humans have lost the knowledge, the secrets of the universe that were brought here by our ancestors of the planets. The cosmic knowledge is the only thing that will help Mother Earth—to have the ceremony on sacred ground, to have Mystery Schools to educate the people, to teach the knowledge of the cosmos. There is no university like that.

This is good news, to have your visit. You are Nancy Red Star, the person of the Red Star people, the Morning Star Venus. This is true, we each have our planet of origination. It is confirmation of the work we are doing. *[Laughing, with an arm raised.]* Yes! This is good news for me! Maybe at one time you can return and we can work directly with the Red Star. Remember, the indigenous of this country are the Red people. Why are we red? There are many colors of people. They each have identification with a planet: the seven brothers of my Father, the seven sisters of my Mother, the seven powers of the body. Like the snake on your equinox map, the sacred number seven forms the snake within the Milky Way.

The seven powers in our spine are a small snake. Our solar system is the large snake, which is connected to the larger snake of the Pleiades. By honoring these we can all connect back with our Star Ancestors and planets of origination. To fulfill the Atlante-Itza prophecy all people all over the world must return to sacred ceremonial centers to acquire the knowledge, or our future on planet Earth will be jeopardized.

The prophetic and scientific book the Popol Vuh warns us that "the Comet" marked the end of an era. In the Popol Vuh it is said that they who came before the Comet advised us that they only came as pilgrim visitors.

At the beginning of this cycle Halley's Comet was seen in the heavens, in 1986. Then other comets, such as Hayakutake, with its tail

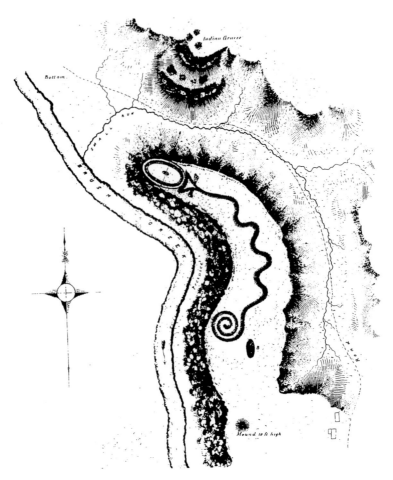

◙ *Serpent Mound*
  Adams County, Ohio, Squier/Davis, 1848

longer than that of any other comet, and Hale-Bopp, with its head as brilliant as Sirius. In 1998 the comet Tempel-Tuttle appeared, perfectly visible from Mayan ceremonial centers. On these occasions the traditional Maya people were very glad to see again the great sign of our All-Powerful Lord, the Comet. The Mayan culture believes that each passing of a comet indicates the end of a cycle. We understand the law of cosmic change. For this reason the Mayan culture, which comes from the Pleiades, was created for all living beings who are encountered in any corner of the universe.

All that exists on Mother Earth has essence as well as spirit. To the Maya, essence and spirit are one and the same, and their never-ending cyclic language tells matter how to act to give way to the cyclic changes. My uncle, Don Beto, explained this to me many years ago in a very simple manner. One day as my uncle and I were walking in the jungle near Espita, my hometown, he suddenly gestured that we sit on some stones that were under a beautiful tree. As we sat down I perceived the aroma of mango fruit. My uncle was watching me and asked if I felt like eating a mango. Then he said, "Today the mango fruit is not present. That is the way of existence; everything arrives spiritually first. Just as the mango fruit arrives, so does everything that exists. That is how we humans arrived in this world, first spiritually and later physically.

"Hunbatz, remember the pyramids at X Wenk'al [in the Yucatan]. That site is sacred to us, the Maya. Our physical roots are in that ancient site, and it was there that our ancestors understood many laws on all that exists from the Great Spirit. In X Wenk'al, as well as in hundreds of pyramids on this continent, our ancestors performed ceremonies to honor all that was visible and not visible. You cannot see the mango fruit, yet you can perceive its aroma."

Then my uncle's expression turned sad. I respectfully asked him the reason for such a change. There was a sad tone in his voice as he answered, "The way things are changing makes me very sad. Modern civilization is losing respect for all that comes from the Great Spirit." He continued, "Many of the animals that I used to see around this jungle are physically gone; the big trees are gone too. Everything is disappearing physically, and my spirit grieves for this reason. I always implore the sacred Hunab'Ku that we are not left without the essence-spirit of all that is gone, and that some day he will again send the physical beauty we no longer see."

In 1994 I was invited to give some lectures in England. While I was in that sacred land I had the privilege of walking on one of the crop formations, one of the many that had been found in wheat fields at various locations in England. When I walked on this one, which had recently been formed near the Avebury pyramid, I could sense the change in the frequency of the energy emitted. I felt as if Mother Earth was emitting energy upward. It is important to note that a group of initiates and myself had, the day before, performed a ritual precisely on that magnetic site, and the crop formation was not there. But it was there the following day, and as we walked on it we entered its dimension. Some people claim that these geometric designs are made by farmers in the area. I am absolutely certain that this formation was not man-made.

When I sat within the formation to meditate I remembered my uncle's teaching of the essence-spirit concept. Then I understood that, through this sacred site, Mother Earth was trying to communicate with intelligent, open-minded human beings who could understand the language of sacred geometry in its mathematical and vibrational aspects.

In 1996 I received a photograph of a recent crop formation in England. The photograph seemed to suggest that the essence and body of our Mother Earth was no longer in the orbit it occupied for many millions of years, and this saddened me. I have carried this photograph to many ceremonial centers; at each sacred site I show it to the Father Sun and sometimes the Sister Moon. When in meditation I send it to the heart of Mother Earth and ask for her advice as to what can be done in order not to lose her essence and her body. I invite every human being to do likewise.

I still remember my uncle's sadness over the animals and trees that were gone, and I too feel sad. When you, Solar Brother and Solar Sister, notice that in the area where you live the animals and trees begin to disappear, you will realize that we are gradually facing isolation. Our life-giving spirits are disappearing. The spirits that support this Blue Planet are being lost to another dimension. Should all essence-spirit be gone, Mother Earth may exhale her last sigh. Without her essence, her body may disappear and we all may pass to the memory of what was once here.

The purpose of the Mayan initiation work through the Mystery

◘ *Palenque*
Oscar Rodriguez, Tarahumara

Schools is to determine what can be done to avoid this—we were sent to this planet to care for it and love it. The Mystery Schools are not new; their purpose and the purpose of humanity exist in our history. By bringing back the idea of the Mystery Schools we are trying to recover all the knowledge we had during the ancient Mayan days. We know the knowledge existed in the past.

Many people can say they know something about the Mayan civilization, but today most of the explanations we have are those of the official education system: archaeological or anthropological studies on how the Maya lived. These books, though, are written in the manner that the Spanish wanted people to see the Maya. When the Spanish invaded they rewrote the story of the Maya; they used a western mentality to explain an ancient culture. The explanations are the same in Mexican universities, and in the United States. People cannot understand the true power of the Mayan culture because the true information was withheld. We need to understand why they rewrote the Mayan history. And we need to know that we, the Mayan traditional people, know our culture.

Creating the Mystery Schools is re-creating our history in order to explain the Mayan civilization from the traditional point of view. In that way the Mayan culture and the knowledge can come to help humanity. Humanity today is making many mistakes, many of which we cannot see. The Mystery Schools are here to awaken human consciousness. They have been created in different countries and in different cultures to explain the teachings of certain ancient ancestors.

I hope in the future that many people from many different cultures can come together through the teachings of the Mystery Schools. For example, when I have a meeting with some Inca people, or Kahuna from Hawaii, we don't have a problem understanding each other. We connect through the ancient teachings. We speak the same language. You see, when people come to the Mystery School they come to seek the knowledge. They come to do the ritual. The rituals are performed in connection with the natural laws, and that is the reason they are so important. We have now some thirty Mystery Schools throughout the world. The only requirement is communication. So if there is some illumination, some message in the cosmos—like Hale-Bopp, for instance—everyone is aware and ready to observe the teachings, the marking of the cycle revealed in the cosmos.

The spiritual education of the people on the planet moves. At one time we had the spiritual education of the people in Mayan land. Then it moved. The Mother Earth indicates where it's going to be. Mother Earth can show us where the power to awaken the consciousness is going to come again.

With all the pollution, the people of Earth today cannot make the connection regarding the real capacity of the cosmic power. The higher beings of other dimensions are different; they work on many levels. They can stop all the electricity here in the city of Merida. They can do that, and they will.

In Maya we call extraterrestrials *muxul*. The muxuls are our Star Guardians; they are the ones who know the end. You see, we know that many things exist, but as humans we don't know the end. For example, we have a small cycle: one day, one month, one year. This is a small cycle. The muxul can tell you of one cycle of thirty thousand years, and what will happen in that cycle. They can tell the future. The muxuls can travel within the dimensions of the past, present, and future.

With the teachings from the muxuls the people of the Mayan civilizations have acquired many powers that modern people cannot understand. For instance, the power of the vibration coming through the crown temple, covering the top of the skull, has a name. That name in Maya is *cizin*. We used to know very well how to work with this power, but when the Christians came they changed *cizin* to *devil*. The power of the crown chakra was converted to an evil symbol. The power of the crown chakra was lost through the Spanish legacy; many Mayas lost the power to use these sacred instruments.

In Maya the word *hopi* means "illumination." I knew Thomas Benyaca, the Hopi elder. He came here to visit two times. We went to Palenque, and he told me that a long time ago the Hopi were in Palenque and made the migration north to Hopiland. This word *hopi* in Maya means the crown chakra. The action when the light comes from the skullcap is *hopi;* it illuminates the crown.

Go to Chichén Itzá. Go to the celestial observatory and look at all the faces of the many people carved in stone. Most of those faces look like humans, but some of the faces are muxul, extraterrestrial. A long time ago the Master Teachers came to that place from another place outside the world to teach about the sky. For instance, take the day of March 16, 1999. In the Mayan calendar, March 16, 1999, will be the day K'an 10, month Uayeb 3, year Chichan 12. The initiate's work will be to have clear judgment, to understand the principle of life in water, which represents the seven powers of the feminine. Having understood, the student becomes a teacher to communicate this awakening. The Master Teachers stayed to teach the people about the cosmos. When you go there, try to identify the faces. You will recognize them.

At noon on March 21, 1999, there will be a very interesting formation of planets. This formation includes the celestial vault of the Pleiades, the Moon, Venus, Saturn, Jupiter, the Sun, and Mercury. These planets are frequently marked in the Mayan codices and on vessels, as well as on the Maya stelae. *[The stelae are great stone monuments marking the passage of cycles in periods of many years.]*

I will summarize the year 1999: To be strong but with maturity and with dual thoughts (masculine, feminine); to be a teacher who directs and creates centers of cosmic teaching; and to be a student, learning from the very ancient cultures.

On this day, through meditation, we will ask to be shown the way and to come to understand the calendar cycles that will enable us to pinpoint our errors. We are invited to learn to adjust our lives in accordance with the sacred Mayan calendar, and to ask Mother Earth what is our cyclic responsibility so we can all live in harmony with the essence-spirit of Mother Earth. This is the only way to preserve the spirit of our planet. We will ask the spirit of all the masters of all times and dimensions, as well as the spirit of all forms of life, to guide us and to be present as essences of solar light.

The whole of humanity today needs the education coming from the cosmos because, as is known, the education of modern civilization is not complying with the universal Creator's correct mandates. The new time will come to correct two thousand years of mistaken direction, to eradicate these thousands of years of darkness.

When the universal memory began to wake up in remote times, there we were with seven corporal and spiritual powers. There are two more powers that we cannot take until we understand and develop the seven powers. One of these two powers is up in the universe, and the other one is below in nature. They are complementary powers to the seven that correspond to our body and spirit.

Inside our memory a great power exists. Accessing our ancestral memory will take us to remote boundaries of our existence. We will remember the lands and religion of the ancient Mother culture. We cannot see them because those great sacred lands are under the waters of the sea. The Maya can remember the last great sacred lands of the continent of Lemuria, or Lemulia, in the Mayan language. Many people inherited the sacred symbols of Lemulia. These symbols were the summary of wisdom; they also represented religion. The symbols were worshipped, not like some religions that commercialize sacred symbols nowadays. In order for humans to understand these symbols, they have to enter into the land of the cosmic initiation.

Some indigenous groups, such as the Hopi, are in the sacred lands of Lemulia. They came from south of the American continent in order to settle in what is the United States of North America. When they arrived here many of the lands were under the sea. The Hopi know in their registered memory the big changes that have occurred to the sacred lands in the north of this American continent.

Every several thousand years the magnetic pole of religion arises in a different part of Earth. The ancient wise men of knowledge travel, taking with them the great power they cared for in order to deposit it in the new location. When this great power indicated by the cosmos and Mother Earth arose in Lemulia, people with high degrees of initiation traveled to help ease the activation of this new sacred place where the spiritual education would arise. Through the passing of the millennia, Lemulia fulfilled its sacred mission as educator of humanity. When the cycle indicated by the Maya calendars was complete, Lemulia returned under the waters of the sea.

The Itzaes of tradition can remember when we were on the continent of Atlantis, or Atlantina, in the Mayan language. In those remote times our sacred symbols were in all the locations of the continent of

Atlantina; those who inhabited these lands could understand these symbols that represented all knowledge of the universe.

When Atlantina arose from the waters of the sea, many teachers came to deposit the sacred wisdom in this place. They came following a cosmic order. The Lemulians were present in order to deposit the great power to the Atlantinans; with rites and ceremonies they made the transition of power. The cycle indicated by the calendars also marked the time when the continent of Atlantina would arrive at its end. When this began to happen, many communities emigrated to other places. The Atlantinan/Itza community also had to emigrate to new lands. This is where the great continent that is today called America arose.

The original name of these sacred lands for us, the Itzaes of tradition, is Tamauanchan. In Mayan, Ta-Mauan-Chan means Land of the Eagle (male) and Land of the Serpent (female): the Americas. The great Tamaunchan arose as a continuer of the cosmic spiritual education ordered by the new magnetic pole. In these sacred lands arose the high initiatic degree of the Mayan language. Here also are the symbols of the snake and the eagle, and the seven powers of the human being. When the initiates comprehended these powers of the body, then they were clever enough to understand the other two complementary powers—the high one of the cosmos and the one under the earth.

So now we face the cosmic change moving us into the new magnetic pole of spiritual education. Let us see with our true human power a little of our cosmic solar memory. In this way we will begin to understand what we have forgotten.

SOLAR INITIATION
OF THE MYSTERY SCHOOLS

Follow the equinox   Follow the solstice   Participate in rituals   To learn ancient teachings   In accordance with solar calendars   Illuminating alignments   Determining the work

Characters of a glyph   Codes for meditation   Decipher the cycles   Preserve the essence-spirit   Of the planet Invoke the masters   Of all times   Of all dimensions   Of all forms

Visitors   Pilgrim travelers   Guide us   Protect us   Crown us   With a language of light   In ecstasy   Activate for ascension   Our galactic conduit   For solar initiation   Into the mystery school

Planetary formation of the Pleiades, the Moon, Venus, Saturn, Jupiter, the Sun, and Mercury will represent the initiate teachings:

Tzek'eb—Pleiades—Rattle of the cosmic serpent. It represents the seven Suns.

Uc—Moon—Forces of the liquids that govern Mother Earth. It represents the seven powers.

Elelek'—Venus—Venus and Earth are like twins. In harmony, both planets coexist and provide each other balance.

Ain Ek'—Saturn—Great change that will bring the waters.

Yaax Ek'—Jupiter—Green will emerge as life. It will create more vegetation.

K'In—Sun—Solar era. People must begin to incorporate solar wisdom into their beings.

Xux Ek'—Mercury—Messenger of life. It makes the body strong so body can radiate light.

8 IT WILL HAPPEN IN HOPILAND

Sacred Site Empowerment

PAUL WERNER DUARTE

> *Those from the Center make us unite*
> *The Eagle of the North and the Condor of the*
>   *South.*
> *We will meet with our Relatives because we*
>   *are One,*
>   *as the fingers of our hand.*
>
> HOPI PROPHECY

At the great Mayan teaching center at Palenque there is an underground passageway, a labyrinth, through which students were made to pass blindfolded. The purpose of the journey was to pass through darkness, as in the underworld, emerging in the light at the outer opening of the temple. The journey was "the awakening," signaling the next life.

My second journey to Mexico sent me down into the dark path of the underworld. My travels became an initiation I had to pass through in order to receive the gifts of knowledge. There were moments in the darkness of this trip when I felt I might not get home; nothing could have prepared me for this twist in my feeling of safety. A powerful presence was affecting my ability to stay centered and surefooted. I was challenged to the depths of my being with the delicacy of carrying the knowledge.

At my final destination in Palenque, Chiappas, I sayed at Hotel Xibalba, which in Mayan means "underworld." I stayed in room 9; nine, the last of the levels of the underworld. This is a literal dimension. Earth has four levels and the heavens have thirteen. I must pass through the nine levels of the underworld—my initiation—to gain the knowledge of our Master Teachers and to enter the light of the next life. —NRS

Paul Duarte's Indian name is Yuk, "Little Deer." He is a German/ Mayan descendant of the Olmec culture from Vera Cruz, Mexico. He was initiated into Olmec medicine ways at age six by his grandmother, Claudina Duarte, a full-blooded Olmec seer. Paul is one of the "new elders," and everywhere he walks bands of children follow him. Fluent in four languages—Yucatec Mayan, German, Spanish, and English—Paul studied anthropology at DePaul University and is currently a federal tour guide in the ancient lands of Mexico. He has been working with the Hopi since 1993. Paul carries the ancient wisdom and knowledge of the Mayan culture.

My interest in the Hopi began in the late 1980s when I was studying in Chicago at DePaul University. I had come upon symbols of the Hopi, Mayan, and Tibetan cultures, and noticed relationship not only in the visual nature of the symbols but also in their meanings and the ways they were used in ceremony. This led me to formulate my thesis that these three cultures came from the same Mother culture.

My studies led me to Arizona, but my time there was cut short by having to move from the States to the Yucatan Peninsula in southern Mexico. I set up home in a village near Chichén Itzá and began to seriously study the Maya.

One evening I got the idea that I should take a Mayan book to the Hopi, not only to further investigate my theory but also to open communication between the Hopi and the Maya. I decided on a book called the Dresden Codex, which is one of the four surviving ancient Mayan books. (The original text is in Dresden, Germany.) This book is basically concerned with the stars and with Venus; it was originally written in Chichén Itzá. I chose another book as well, one I had bought in Palenque. This book was specifically about the Temple of Inscriptions and Lord Pacal.

I decided to move back to Arizona to live for a couple of months out of the year, and took these two books with me. I headed to Hopiland blindly, not having any connection to the people there. I went to Walpi, one of the mesas. The day I arrived they were having a dance—one for

◩ *Paul Werner Duarte*
  Olmec, Chiapas, Mexico

the tourists, not a sacred dance. I was treated like a *pa-hana,* a White man. I was reduced to tears. I literally sat on the ground at the mesa and cried.

When a Zuni Sun Clan Mother asked why I was crying I explained to her that I had come all the way from the land of the Maya to bring these two books to someone who could find relevance in them and the Hopi culture. She asked me if I would like to meet a person who had been working with the Tibetans, specifically with the Dalai Lama. I said I would, but I requested that she not mention the books. I stood with her while she made the phone call, and was then invited to the home of Thomas Pela, younger son of Earl Pela, one of the last blood-lineage leaders of the Hopi. Tom had been entrusted by his father and the elders, the Kikmongwi (the Holy Men), with a plethora of information. Being an official spokesman for the traditional Hopi, Tom Pela travels all over to deliver the Hopi prophecy to those who will listen.

Upon reaching the house of Tom Pela's girlfriend in Moenkopi, I knocked on the door. Tom answered. He looked me over and smiled. His first question was "Where is the book?" even though the Zuni woman had mentioned nothing about the book to him. This brought a smile to my face. I gave Tom the Dresden Codex. Tom read the book by putting his palm over it to absorb the knowledge. After some minutes Tom thanked me and said that the book had relevance to the Hopi but not to his clan, the Sun Clan.

Then he smiled and said, "Where is the other book?" I began to laugh and handed him a book with a picture of the jade mask of Lord Pacal, the Lord of Palenque, on the cover. This picture brought tears to Tom's eyes. He asked if the mask was turquoise. I explained that it was jade and that, to the Maya, jade has the same significance as turquoise does to the people of Hopiland. As he put his hand down to absorb the knowledge of this book Tom appeared no longer to be there with us. He rocked back and forth singing ancient songs. He opened his medicine bundle and he took out three stones. He called them his dolphin stones. They were a gift from the Maori people of New Zealand, who reached him first in the dreamtime and then physically came to visit.

When Tom regained his composure he explained to me that, ever since he was a child, his father told him that one day he would get a visit from someone who would bring a book. This book would be from Paletkwapi, which is the Hopi name for the "ancient red city of the South": Palenque. His father had warned that the person bringing the book would not physically look like the person Tom might anticipate. As I am a six-foot mixed-blood with shoulder-length hair, not of the physical type that one would expect to see from the southern jungles, Tom considered my visit to be the fulfillment of his father's prophecy.

Tom asked if there was something I needed to request of him. He thought I had a lot heaviness on my shoulders and in my heart. For the next three or four hours Tom patiently listened to the stories of my journeys in Mexico and the tribulations I had endured. When I finished he explained to me again that they had waited a long time; now that the meeting had begun between the Maya and the Hopi, the focus was on Palenque. This was the beginning of the end. The old cycles are finishing and the new cycles are coming. This gathering, the meeting of the cultures, was meant to happen. He invited me to come back to Hopiland in a week or two, when I felt ready. We were to meet for a deeper connection. In the Hopi tradition one goes through initiation before a teacher officially begins working with someone such as myself.

So I went home for a couple of weeks. Soon I felt it was time to go back to Hopiland. Once again, no one knew when I was coming. There was no official communication; I just showed up. I went dressed in Mayan white and wearing a red headband—my traditional clothing. Again I had to go to the village of Moenkopi. This time Tom picked me up at two o'clock in the morning and settled me into the back of a station wagon. I had blankets put over me and bags of groceries put on top of them. Then I was driven up to Second Mesa, where Tom lives, and was snuck inside his house.

Tom set a sleeping bag on the floor and asked me to get myself into the dream state. He and Radford Quamahongnewa, the Snake Priest, along with the Kikmongwi, the spiritual leader, were going to the kiva. They were going to meditate and to "smoke" me, to see what I was about. I agreed.

In the predawn hours we made contact in the dream state. A few hours later I was awakened by Tom coming back to his house with Radford. He explained to me that, being a Snake Priest, Radford was not apt to have a lot of time to speak, and assured me that I shouldn't feel bad if I only had ten minutes with him. Radford stayed until Sun break. I invited them to a gathering I was planning in Mexico—a visit to the sacred pyramids, for the purpose of speaking of the past, the present, and the future with the Mayan spiritual leaders. Radford had been waiting for this invitation.

I left Arizona. Until that point I had been traveling with two stones, a round quartz and a square pyrite. When the burial place of Pacal was found he had in his right hand a square stone and in his left hand a round stone, representing the male and the female balance. I was given the pyrite, which had been found in the hand of a skeleton sticking out of the ground in Palenque. An indigenous person had given this to me. I had brought these stones from Mexico to Arizona to show them to a Hopi spiritual leader, but suddenly I couldn't find them. When I told Tom about the disappearance he laughed and said, "Your stones are waiting for you in your house in Mexico. It's time for you to go back to Mexico." Since the time I was young I've experienced supernatural powers and witchcraft at the feet of my grandmother. I strongly believe in such powers, but this was hard to swallow.

I made my way back to Mexico, but once at home I couldn't find the stones. Then one evening I was looking for one of my rare books in a storage room. I was digging through the piles of books and found

◘ *Lord Pacal*
Oscar Rodriguez, Tarahumara

the one I was looking for. As I lifted it up I saw my stones underneath. The pyrite and the quartz had traveled by themselves back to Mexico. Tom knew this, so now my trust level was starting to build. I would contact him periodically at his girlfriend's to receive advice. He was advising me very well—never giving me the secrets, only the clues. He let me learn on my own.

Eventually during a meditation in Chichén Itzá I saw Tom materialize within a lavender light. I knew the time had come for me to see him again. When I arrived back in Arizona an older couple was waiting for me. They were very deeply involved with UFO activity and had an international group for contactees. The group studied cases from all over the world to compare experiences. After staying with them for some days I felt clear enough to proceed on to Hopiland. I arrived and was received by Tom, his girlfriend, and her three daughters.

I slept well that night. Tom told me to relax, that we would not discuss anything until we went to Second Mesa. The next morning, once again beneath blankets in the back of the car, I was taken up to Tom's house. Again I knew that, for Tom, there would only be trouble if I was seen dressed in my whites and my red headband up in that area. If the nontraditionals saw me coming to Tom they would surely reproach him about it. Tom has a lot of trouble there. He leaves an obsidian dagger at his door, declaring that if anyone wants to kill him they can do so with the obsidian knife.

Tom explained to me that it was important I understood my role in the unfolding progress of relations between the Mayan people and the Hopi. Why was I here with him? Why was he treating me like a brother? Why was I seeing him in visions at the temples of Mexico? Why the books about Palenque? He explained to me that many, many generations back, in the fog of time, the Hopi had emerged in the Second World in Palenque. In my past life I had also emerged from this place, and had been there for the formation of the six clans. I had made the migration to Hopiland. At this time I was a custodian, a caretaker at Na Chan (Palenque). I was a watcher at Na Chan for the Maya and Hopi, caretaking the trail that was made so long ago.

Tom told me that one place of emergence was near a certain temple with two rivers nearby. He gave me tobacco and two quartz stones, one rose and one amethyst, and told me that when I went back to Mexico I was to find this place in the jungle.

At this point Tom asked me to take a walk with him in the desert. He said this could be dangerous considering the situation; however, I wanted to go with him and recognize in public the connection we had made. So we broke our secrecy to walk to the rock at Oraibi, the Prophecy Stone. This large stone in the desert carries an inscription of two paths coming out from the First World. It shows Massau, the godhead, with his planting stick. It also shows the two paths that people

◼ *Mudhead Katsina*
  Duane O'Hagan

will take. The false path is very rocky with many ascents and descents, many trials and tribulations. The true path is a straight line that is cut off at the end. These are the two roads we are now on. Tom explained to me that he is the caretaker for the emergence of the First World. This is his responsibility.

That night I accompanied Tom to the airport. He was flying to Austin. We were near Flagstaff, somewhere around Oak Creek Canyon, when I asked Tom if he had ever seen any lights in the sky. He said "Yes, the Katsinas. They brought us here. They have watched over us always and we have never lost contact. One day they will come back. They are our brothers. We are them, and they are us."

At this point the person driving said there was a light up ahead near the mountain. Tom began laughing with glee when the light moved up fast, zooming to behind us. Suddenly there was a light in back of the car. Then Tom pointed to the right. One hundred yards away was a cigar-shaped craft with a twirling neon light on one side. Tom was beginning to laugh more and more. He pointed out the window to the left. There was another craft, this one triangular in shape. I could see the light of the triangle.

Tom told me to watch. The craft started changing its design, changing the lights from triangle to circle to square. Tom told me they were "teaching geometry." He was like a kid; I was in awe, as was the person driving. This continued for ten minutes. We had twenty-five craft above us at one time. Then suddenly a gigantic light came out of the mountain. It seemed to explode into sparks, and each spark of light became a craft that flew in its own way, its own formation. Yet at no point did the cigar-shaped craft leave us, nor did the triangular-shaped craft leave.

We had a symphony of lights all around us. The round ones were familiar to me. We call them the "cosmic tow trucks" in Chichén Itzá because they have round blinking lights; they look like jellyfish from beneath. This continued on for some time, then the crafts started disappearing one by one. You don't really see them leave. One minute they are there and the next minute they're gone. You never see a trajectory.

Tom turned to me and asked, "Do you have any other questions?" Basically, this was his gift to me.

That was the last time I saw Tom Pela. Before he left for Austin that day he told me a huge earthquake starting in the San Andreas fault will make a U-shaped divide through the United States. The divide will be several miles wide and will extend through the southern region all the way up to New York state. This fault line will split the mesas at Hopiland, making it difficult to get from First Mesa to Second Mesa or Second Mesa to Third Mesa. The gap will be miles wide and miles deep. Tom said the Kikmongwi will knock on doors and ask, "Do you know your language? Do you know your culture? Do you know your ceremonies? Do you know your dances?" Those who know these things will go to one ceremonial platform. The people who don't will be taken to another platform, and the earth will continue to open. The two peoples will be separated forever. Only the people who keep the traditions, who keep their promise to Massau, the Creator, will remain. Those who kept the promise will be removed by the Katsinas and protected; those who have not will see the dark night of tribulation. Without maintaining the traditions we will have a long, long time of darkness. The path is the goal.

Tom said that, in ancient times, there was a ship that was composed of seven pieces—six pie-shaped sections and one round section in the middle. When the Hopi arrived on Atlantis the ship split up; each of the six pie-shaped ships went to a sacred place in the world. We spoke about those different locations—obviously the Himalayas and in Peru—where these ships might be. Tom made it obvious that one of the pieces rested in Palenque. The main hub, the middle piece, is in the San Francisco Peaks, which is where the Hopi say the Katsinas live. When the time comes these ships will all meet again in Hopiland and the vehicle will be put back together. This is the way the people will be removed for the future generations. They will watch the tribulations to form our new stories.

According to Tom, the neon light of the cigar-shaped craft was giving information activating our genes. Humans today have a double helix form of DNA; what science calls DNA is simply two strands of genetic material that intertwine. But we also have "junk DNA," extra DNA. Science has not figured out the purpose of this DNA. The Hopi taught me that humans used to have twelve strands—not two but twelve. The Popul Vuh, the ancient Mayan book, says that ancient man and woman could see everywhere, they could know everything. They could communicate with each other by thought. In the ancient times people did not talk, they sang. The light did not come from the Sun and the Moon, it came from inside the body.

A neutrino is a fundamental particle that is constantly passing through Earth from space. This is energy; this light passing through our bodies is like a harmonic convergence. Everything happens through light. Everything is light. Everything. The point is: we are no longer working in the way we were built. Our systems have been taken apart so that we can no longer see everywhere. We can no longer hear everything. We can no longer read through our minds, which was common practice in ancient times. When I was driving with Tom Pela and the lights were shooting from the craft, he said to me, "They are awakening your genes, your memories. Your twelve-strand helix will reconnect. That is the essence of true being." This all happens through light.

Now, as light and light beings are connecting our DNA, we are getting abductions at the same time. This is where the Greys come in, the ETs who have been doing genetic experimentation on humans. They are the ones who disconnected us. In every kind of being there is good and bad—duality. Forty thousand years ago certain ETs began manipulating the human genetic system, taking away ten strands of our DNA to create modern man, a workforce breed. The Greys are now taking the DNA that has been reconnected and using that to create hybrids. This is really what's going on behind the cloning and the genetic research today. In the underground laboratory where this hybridizing is being carried out, the negative entities are reconnecting the strains to make a workforce for the battle. There is an intergalactic conflict currently raging.

When I talk about the Greys I refer to the ones who have not helped us, those who have these underground laboratories and work in collusion with the government. They are the ones who abduct us and treat us harshly, like cattle. There is a great difference between visitors and abductors. A lot of the abduction scenarios are not very friendly. If you look at the face of an insect you'll see the face of a Grey. I would never speak of canceling out an entire race, but we can say that the Greys are desperate to continue their species.

If you look at ancient time lines you will notice that, at the same time you have a high culture, like Atlantis, you also have Neanderthals. At the same time you have Lemuria you have Australopithecus, the Stone Age people. This is Big Foot, Sasquatch, the ancestor of man. He is not a true man yet. He is an interdimensional being, one who survived for thirty-five thousand years. He has not been fully disconnected.

◘ *Face of a Grey*
Stan Neptune, Penobscot

He can appear in dreams, and he can materialize and then disappear. Sasquatches don't live in the same reality we do; you only see them when they want you to see them.

There is an entire race of Sasquatches. They live in caves. We live right now on the porch of Earth. The planet is three parts water and one part earth. The inside of Earth is three parts land and one part water. This is where many beings live. I have been with the Maza Tec near Oaxaca, Mexico. They are famous for their stories of Don Juan. The Maza Tec told me that in the mountains of Oaxaca there is an entrance to a city that is in the earth. The people that have been fortunate enough to find it never come back. They don't want to leave. It is like Shambhala, a Shangri-La, paradise.

The inside of Earth is inhabited. This is why we don't see Sasquatches in the forest all the time. Those who are familiar with the folklore of the indigenous people of the Americas know that they do not have violent experiences with Big Foot. The indigenous people don't fear him. Big Foot is seen as someone with whom they can communicate. In the modern world there have been violent interactions. In Montana, for instance, four Sasquatches attacked some people in a cabin. These loggers had hunted a young male Sasquatch through the forest. Later that evening four male Sasquatches came—remember, they are eight or nine feet tall—and they started tearing down the walls of the cabin. In fact, one Sasquatch cut his hand. The loggers found a clump of bloody hair, which they sent off to be analyzed. The evidence showed that the hair came from a species never before cataloged on Earth. Such facts are specifically kept from the public.

The Sasquatch is an ancient relation, one that is keeping to the original tradition. The Yeti, the indomitable snowmen of the Himalayas, are cousins to the Sasquatch. Sir Edmond Hillary, the first man to climb Mount Everest, took pictures of Yeti tracks. Hillary asked his sherpas about the tracks and was told they belonged to an ancient, ancient being that has survived throughout the generations. If you speak to a Tibetan lama he will talk of the Yeti as a reality, not as a legend. Earth has gone through so many generations that the fairies, the gremlins, the trolls, the leprechauns, the water beings, the Sasquatch all have gone into hiding. Modern men and women no longer believe in them. Is there any pain worse than being ignored, or not being believed in? This is why the Sasquatch can't be seen. They are in the Redwoods, in the Himalayas, in the ancient, ancient places where they can still hide from modern man.

There are many species: the Greys, the Katsina people, the Nordics, the Angelics. The Nordics are the blonde people most likely from Pleiades. They, together with the Angelics, have always been interested in our development on Earth. They are the ones who are not interested in dominating us. They are larger men and women who look like us, with lighter skin and blonde hair or dark hair. They have been helping us since the beginning. These beings have always been with us. There are possibly as many races as there are stars.

The Red man has had a covenant with the beings from space since the beginning. The Red man is the Atlantean. Edgar Cayce once said, "Take an Aztec, take a Maya, take a Hopi, take a Cherokee, take a Cheyenne, and you're looking at an Atlantean." This is the closest you'll ever come to seeing an Atlantean. The Atlanteans were the Red people. Atlantis was a high culture—as was Lemuria—the knowledge having been brought from our home in space.

Earth is not the original home for any human race. Earth is a big terrarium, and the atmosphere has been made for us. This is the reason that, as NASA goes looking for life elsewhere, scientists say that other planets don't have the correct atmosphere for us, for carbon-based beings. Other beings need other atmospheres.

The Red man descended to Earth from the Pleiades; indigenous people have a long history of space exploration and extraterrestrial contact. In Mexico, where I am a citizen, we are not allowed in the sites at night, even as federal tour guides, because there is so much craft activity at the temple sites. Craft visit the pyramids almost every night.

In Guatemala they land, they come out, and they talk with the people. This is normal; it's not a rare event. When these beings arrive they adjust themselves to the culture. If they land with the Maya they will adjust to looking like an ancient Maya. They are shapeshifters. That is the kind of transformation they can make. We can do this too, when we are realized. We are light, not hard material. We are sound.

In the ancient days the hieroglyphs were created to foretell the future, the awakening. These writings were created as codes of a secret history with ancient astronauts. In the future, when people programmed from the old times come in contact with these glyphs those symbols will awaken their genetic systems. This is why the glyphs are important. They were created as a security system. It's important to do ceremonies and to meditate upon these glyphs. You will find some glyphs that you feel very close to and others that don't mean anything to you. This is a safety net that we left for ourselves many eons ago. We knew our cycle, and we all knew that we were going to spend time in the Dark Ages. We knew that we were going to forget our divinity, who we really are, so we put up these safety nets for ourselves. As we say in Mayan culture, when you are becoming reconnected you are becoming a real man or real woman. This is very important, because when your original DNA is reconnected you become a true cosmic being.

Much important information has been removed from the sacred sites. The Vatican has one of the four remaining Mayan manuscripts. The Vatican has a telescope on the Apache sacred mountain. Why? I believe these covenants between Star Beings and humans were made a long time ago, and certain points on Earth were picked to be watchtowers. We were told to watch in the skies for occurrences. When these occurrences take place they mark the time of return, the time of the passing of cycles. That is why the Vatican has an interest in the Apache sacred mountain. Another area of interest to the Vatican is down near Machu Picchu, another is the Serpent Mound in Ohio. There is much interest in mass landings, because once they happen the economic, political, and religious structures will never be the same. There are many who want to be the first to see the signs from the skies, the occurrence.

The code—the true history, knowledge, and wisdom of our travel to other dimensions and contact with other beings—those teachings still remain in the Mayan language. Look at the name Chichén Itzá. *Chi* means "mouth," *chen* is "well," *itza* is "water wizard"—the mouth of the well of the water wizard. The Wizards of the Water People—the Itza—are the Atlanteans. The temples themselves are portals built specifically over doorways to other dimensions. Mayan cities are built to mark the zones of these time portals. A pyramid here in Mexico is a man-made mound; the temple is always built on top, to be closer to the sky and also for the secrecy of the sacred initiation. The pyramid is big because the structure is built over five or six preexisting structures.

Some of the pyramids are hollow inside to store craft. We also believe that the main pyramid in Chichén Itzá, called the Temple of Ku-Kul-Can, may well have been built for a diamond-shaped craft. We only see the top part revealed; however, I have spoken with many older Maya and they talked of the entire building being a craft. After the landing these Maya say that the stones were built around the diamond-shaped craft. So as Tom Pela told me, this place of emergence is here as well as the new place we will be entering—the *vitz,* the sacred mountain. We will find the *pibna,* home of the cave. This is where we will go in.

The Maya have told us in their writings why they put an altar in a certain place, or the reasons why they put a pyramid in a certain place. When they build the temples with sacred geometry they are amplifying the energy of that portal. Sacred geometry, such as a square representing the male and the circle representing the female, is used. In the Mayan culture the god Hunab is the master of everything that can be measured, everything that can be weighed. His symbol is a square with a circle in it. This is sacred geometry; the symbol itself gives a teaching. These shapes are also the building blocks used to create our reality.

So these pyramids, these temples, amplify the doorways to other dimensions, making the passage easier. The Maya never closed off doorways with anything but fabrics; this way the shapes of the building on

◼ *Snake and Egg*
Stan Neptune, Penobscot

the inside could change at will. Inside each temple is a pibna—the first cave, the holiest of holies. This is the smallest temple within the temple, the portal of the portal. You go into the pibna, tie up your blanket, and go on your vision quest. This is when you leave the dimensions you know or you invite other beings to come to you and discuss other realities with you. This is not a mythology, this is not a philosophy—this is the reality to this day.

The university of cosmic knowledge teaches the student how to die correctly. In order to die correctly you must practice sleeping. When you go to sleep you lose consciousness, then you reawaken in what the Tibetans call the luminosity. Your mind creates a reality—we know this as a dream. When you die, the same thing happens. You lose your consciousness and your soul wakes up in the luminosity, and then your mind creates another reality. Then you wander in what the Tibetans call the *bardo,* the in-between state. The Maya would practice dying every night when they went to sleep. They would go to sleep but they would not pass out. They would remain conscious as their bodies fell asleep. Then they would practice going through the bardos, the in-between worlds.

For the Maya, when the time comes to physically leave the body, like a great warrior, you choose the moment that your inner fire will absorb all your essence. You do not leave death to chance. A great warrior picks the day of his death and consciously leaves. In the Tibetan tradition a lama's body will sometimes remain sitting up for six months after he is dead. There will be no decay and there will be rainbows around the body and it will smell like incense or roses. These are the lessons, the last lessons the lamas are giving to the people on Earth. The Maya way is no different.

That is why meditation is so important. Your entire life is about the moment of your death. At the moment of your death—if you know how to die, if you know how to work your way through the underworld, through the bardo system—then you can choose your next cosmic life. Dying isn't easy! Walking through the underworld in the temple is the training for the student in practicing how to die so that, at the moment you die, you are good at directing yourself.

A practice known today as cranial deformation by anthropologists was carried out by the Maya in the higher lineage. When a newborn baby was recognized as someone who would be an astronomer or a mathematician, or would aspire to be a leader or shaman, his head would be placed between two pieces of wood in a triangular shape. The apparatus was left in place for hours every day, until the skull grew into that shape. When the baby's hair began growing, all but the hair at the top of the head would be cut. So the little baby's head actually looked like an ear of corn. The Maya legend says that the Creator made man out of cornmeal and blood. This shaping of the skull was a tribute, honoring that we come from corn.

After death the person's head would be separated from the body, smeared with honey, and put in the forest. The insects would eat the flesh away. The body was burned and the ashes were used in the corn and bean fields, for two purposes—to genetically keep your people with you and to fertilize your crop. This is a way to keep your people always there to help you. The skulls themselves were preserved in a special area.

We believe that after the Maya used cranial deformation, the Peruvians, the Egyptians, the Tibetans, and North American indigenous peoples copied the head of Pacal to awaken the third eye. The reason we believe it was done in Mexico City was to emulate Pacal Kin, the spiritual leader of the Maya. Pacal arrived out of nowhere with his mother, White Quetzal, and his wife, Lady Lotus Flower. After thousands of years of female leadership Pacal became the male leader; his mother had trained him from the time he was thirteen. Pacal arrived with the skull deformation. He was an original Star Ancestor, coming from space to Atlantis and then eventually to Mexico.

The Olmec people came from Atlantis and built temples in Vera Cruz. At the time of the sinking of Atlantis the royal families were removed. The reason Pacal's bones have been kept in a five-ton slab tomb was to always secure his place for him. They built the tomb and then the pyramid around it to make sure nothing was pulled out of there. This is the major portal, very active even today.

Here in our area the Lacondon say that, up until the 1940s, the Tu ho hani, the extraterrestrials, walked freely in the jungle. The Lacondon had free communication with the extraterrestrials. My friend Kin Garcia's father was Chan-Kin, "Small Sun." He lived to be one hundred forty years old. Chan-Kin told his son that after the 1940s the extraterrestrials left. Up until that time the extraterrestrials had communicated with the people. They taught of the stars, of radiation, and the sunspots. The Tu ho hani taught the Lacondon to study Venus and use its cycle to measure the sunspots. Venus revolves around the Sun in 224.7 days. As seen from Earth, which revolves around the Sun on a larger orbit and at a lower speed, Venus returns to the same position with respect to Earth after 584 days. The Lacondon were told that when we start losing sunspots we will begin to receive radiation. The Lacondon were told to measure so many cycles of Venus and then to go into the ground, for the earth will protect them from the radiation.

◻ *Kin Garcia with Paul Duarte,*
Tula

The extraterrestrials also taught the Lacondon to use metal in their headdresses. The Lacondon traded for silver with the Peruvians to cover three special places on the skull—the front where the third eye is, the side of the head just above the ear, and the back of the skull behind the third eye—to protect the hemispheres of the brain. By protecting themselves in this manner they could avoid contamination from the radiation. They could avoid eliminating their race, avoid genetic extinction.

This is what may have happened to this race of space beings, the Tu ho hani. They came to warn us; this is written on the walls here in Na Chan, Palenque. The numbers of the large sunspot cycles; the exact number of days of these large cycles when the sunspots disappear according to the cycles of Venus—it is all written. This is why Venus is so important to the Maya. You have 584 days in the cycle of Venus, and every 117 cycles of Venus the sunspots start leaving. Every large cycle—1,170 cycles of Venus—the sunspots completely disappear, and civilization on Earth is usually wiped out. If you look on a time line from Babylonia to Egypt and you calculate the sunspot cycles, you will see when that civilization goes under. It is when the full radiation of the Sun is hitting Earth that the population drops drastically. This is what the Mayan calendar warns about the year 2012—it is the end of the large cycle that started in 3113 BC.

This is the warning. The Lacondon are the last pure Mayan ancestors. They wear pure white, their hair is long, and their heads are shaped larger. They are the closest living remnants to the Mayan culture. The Lacondon have already started storing food and water underground for the purging time.

The Maya mark the beginning of the Fourth World with the birth of Venus. People ask how a planet can be born. In 3113 BC Venus entered our atmosphere as a comet. All the ancient cultures saw it. Thus, all of their symbols were in relation to Venus: sometimes a man with a beard or a being with a tail. Venus made physical contact with Earth—two or three times it hit. This is not only a Mayan teaching. You will find the same teaching in Peru, in Tibet, in China, and in Babylonia. They all mark 3113 BC as the birth of Venus.

The word *maya* in Sanskrit means "illusion." This is the paradox of this whole experience: while the process is happening, it isn't happening too. *Ma* is the ancient Mayan word for deer, and the suffix "a" relates to water. So Maya is the deer that walked across the water. Our ancestors were the Atlanteans who came across the ten islands of water. The mother of Buddha, her name was Maya. A deer can travel at the speed of lightning through the woods without hurting a plant. So the Atlanteans came a great distance without damaging the environment.

The modern Maya who live in the mountains of Chiappas perform the ceremonies, especially the sweatlodge or *temazcal,* purification of place. This is where the children are born. When a child is brought into the world it is very important to do it in the sweatlodge because it is very, very pure. The smoke, the vapor, is transporting the child's essence from the other worlds to bring him here. The reason that copal is used in the ceremony is because it becomes an *itz,* a type of magical substance that can transport you. We fill our plaza with ceremony of

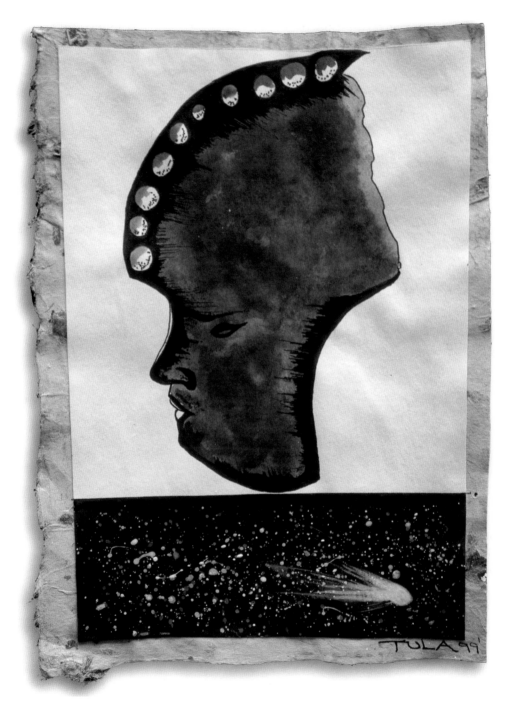

 Flathead (Lives Outside the Third Dimension)
Tula, Abenaki/Cherokee

◘ *Deer Dancer*
Armond Lara, Navajo

copal smoke, making it a magical ocean. This makes it easy for beings to come in and out of dimensions. Even the modern Maya brings his child into being in the clouds.

In the university today in Na Chan on the exterior walls you see four concentric squares. On the outside squares are the beginning knowledge; as you move toward the center you find the higher knowledge. Evidence of craft that have visited the Maya is on the walls. Painted on the wall is a spacecraft as you would see it if you were standing directly under it, as well as a side view of the craft. You can see the landing apparatus, you can see the pod. As you have seen today, also on the walls is a painting of a Mudhead Katsina, as the Hopi have.

The inner square of the university is what is considered by the Mayas to be the highest teachings. Many layers of stucco cover the craft that were painted, so this is very ancient knowledge. What was painted over is from the generations that followed. The looters and archaeologists have given us the true knowledge by destroying the layers on top. These original paintings can be from thirteen to forty thousand years old.

The last people who came to Na Chan came twelve thousand five hundred years ago, from the last Ice Age, the last sinking of Atlantis. The royal families split up from the house of Atlan. Atlan is one of the ten islands; the name Atlantis comes from Atlan Ti-Ha. The Aztec claim their ancestors came from Atz lan. The families left to preserve the teachings traveled in special spacecraft, for the original Atlanteans were from another world. The craft were always available to the Atlanteans. They knew the islands were sinking so they sent the craft to transport their people to different places. From the center they went in six different directions.

The academics, the universities, the archaeologists want people to believe that Atlantis was a myth. They want people to believe the knowledge inscribed in the temples does not forecast a calendar of events that we are now facing. Our civilization professes to be the most advanced; however, we true Maya know this to be false. We know of our ancestors who traversed space, who taught us the highest level of knowledge on the planet. It was the Atlanteans from fifty thousand years ago, when Atlantis started sinking, who built the first pyramids in Egypt. They built the first pyramids in Peru. In Peru there are the Nazca lines that can only be seen from the sky; they represent star constellations. There is also a very large being painted on the side of a mountain. These are for the space people, the people from the sky. The knowledge of levitation, of moving stones, was from the Sky People. Each stone in the Nazca lines weighs 120 tons. The stones were brought from 120 miles away. No cement was used. The stones were cut in a grooved fashion so perfectly that today you cannot put a blade of grass between the stones.

The most important thing to know is that the Star Beings hid this knowledge. In the future, which is still our future, three different writings will appear on three different places on Earth, telling the history of life on and off this planet. This is yet to come. It will reveal itself very soon. One place is the sacred library of Hermes under the great pyramid in Egypt. One is here in Na Chan, Palenque, in the jungle; and the other one is under water. We know these teachings are not written on paper. They may be made on quartz, they may be stone tablets. These beings have been seen flying out of the lagoon in Coba in Quintana Roo, near Tulum. Today the modern Maya see craft flying out of the lagoon at night, out of the water and into the sky. The cities of Atlantis are still under the water. They may rise again. For now they are still being visited, and so are we.

We have been told to prepare. Now is the time.

SACRED SITE EMPOWERMENT

Empowerment of sacred sites   Portals of time   Doors to the universe
Illuminating rays   Of cosmic intelligence   Awaken the pyramids
Reunite knowledge with spirit   Essence with spirit   Human with
being   Space with being

Walk the ziggurats   Limitless steps   Up into the channels   Squares of
genetic memories   Ancient days   Hieroglyphs   Foretelling the future
The awakening

See everything   Hear everything   Call the luminosity   Into your
heartbeat   Meditate upon the glyphs   Codes of symbols   Painted on
walls   Shapes of reality   Pictographs of history   Singing   Not talking

The light   Coming from you   Outward   The Sun   The Moon   The
essence-spirit   Within your solar system   Within your Milky Way
Within your luminosity

Balancing the tilt   Moving from the Fifth World   To the Sixth
World   The new cycle   For all beings   Within our solar system   A
new planetary alignment   Moving into place   Power for a new
Earth   Power from the heavens   Opening the stargate   The changing
of the guard   Marking the new millennium

9 THE PARADIGM SHIFT

We Are All Star Seed

CECILIA VINDIOLA DEAN

> *When all the trees have been cut down,*
> *When all the animals have been hunted,*
> *When all the waters are polluted,*
> *When all the air is unsafe to breathe,*
> *Only then will you discover you cannot eat*
>   *money. . . .*
>
> CREE PROPHECY

Spiritual wisdomkeepers around the world have seen signs occurring, signs that were predicted by ancient prophecies. This has signified the Time Keepers that they must speak their closely held sacred knowledge: our origin from the Star nations; the influence of visitation on the formation of culture, tradition, and ceremony; and the imminent return of our Star Ancestors. Our history with extraterrestrial life is of global significance at this time. The emergence of peace is upon us—the Hopi call this the Fifth World. Knowledge of Star nations is now to be shared.

The Masters of the Stars are frequenting the skies of Mexico, moving north toward the Southwest. Stargate International has not only documented the frequent appearance of these craft but continue to lobby Congress and the United Nations to release government statistics documenting the records of these visitations over the past fifty years.

As I watch and listen to Mother Earth I feel the pace quickening. The lapses in time between natural disasters is brief. Tornadoes, earthquakes, fires, and hurricanes are outside our doors, as predicted. In keeping with the prophecy, before we enter an era of peace we view the Earth changes, staying the course of the mystery that is before us. The teachings are our guide to carry a light of hope into a world of darkness. —NRS

Cecilia Dean worked for seven years as a victim-witness advocate for the Pima County attorney's office, providing crisis response counseling for victims of violent crime. She received her B.A. at the University of Arizona and continued her studies doing graduate

work at Bernard Baruch, City University of New York. She is a member of the Mutual UFO Network (MUFON), a member of the Ancient Astronauts Society, and a member of the Center for the Study of Extra-terrestrial Intelligence (CSETI). She is also a founding member and chief executive officer of Stargate International, a research and educational development organization dedicated to establishing public forums and training programs and creating classroom curricula in the area of UFO history and extraterrestrial intelligence. Cecilia, a powerful, dynamic woman, is of Yaqui descent.

The word *mexican* was originally *mexicano* in Spanish. This was from the Aztec, meaning "half-breed" or "mixed blood." *Mestiso* is the word for half-breed in Spanish, from the Castillian. *Chicano* also comes from the Aztec *mexicano*.

When the Spaniards came to Mexico they carried their language with them. The culture that later became the Mexican culture was a product of intercultural marriages. The Spaniards intermarried with every tribe of the local Indian people—the Oaxaca, Yaqui, Navajo, Comanche, and many others such as the Aztec, Maya, Toltec, and Olmec. The product of these mixes is the Mexican. So a true Mexican will always be a mixed blood because that it what *mexican* means.

My mixed blood—the indigenous part of me—is Yaqui, but there are many other Mexicans whose indigenous blood is something else. When you ask someone, "What Indian background do you have?" there are many answers. I'm not Mexican and something else. Being Mexican is being part Spaniard and part Indian. Mexicans *are* the half-breeds. The full-blooded Yaqui live on the reservation and practice the old ways of our culture—the dances, the ceremonies, the prayers.

■ *Cecilia Vindiola Dean*
Yaqui, Arizona

Here in Tucson the entire Hispanic population is Mexican with a background in either Yaqui or Pima/Maricopa or Tohono O'odnam, which is Papago. We have here a great mixture of Mexicans, as well as Maya and Aztec.

I was born and raised here and my grandmothers were both here when Tucson was still part of Mexico. In 1914, Tucson was part of the Gadsden Purchase. One morning my grandmother woke up and went from being Mexican to being American. Her advice to us was, "They should learn our language. They are the aliens. They are the strangers." Until the day she died she refused to learn English. That was not her language. That was not what was spoken here.

When I think about the Indian prophecies of the cleansing, the purification, I think that this is too mild a word. I call it genocide. Earth is being used to do the cleansing, to commit the genocide. Look at the "chemical trails"—the tic-tac-toe and X-patterns in the sky. These are not vapor trails; they are chemical residues from the aerial experiments on weather manipulation. This is biowarfare—it is a campaign to eliminate part of the world's population. Earth, in and of herself, could probably sustain the population we have because she is so rich in resources. This planet could sustain the population it has if everything was distributed evenly. However, the ruling powers have always wanted and needed much more than their share of the resources. In order for them to continue to live the lifestyles they are accustomed to they have to eliminate a large portion of the population around the world. To me, that is genocide.

Look at Guatemala, Honduras, Colombia, the homelands of indigenous populations. These places are ley lines and earthquake cracks, the fault lines. Wherever the earth is cracked or has a fault line and there is underground testing done, even contained testing, you have a domino effect on the tectonic plates. At some point the results of these tests will have a cumulative effect, and bingo! The fault will open and go around the world. It's not Mother Earth acting on her own. She responds to what is being done to her.

As a human race we have been used to constructing religious belief systems that are very primitive but that sustain us through hard times. There has been no honesty about releasing a much higher teaching, a more evolved approach to religion and to God. We have been given teachings in their most primitive forms. For example, the story of Moses and the burning bush to me is about technology. A voice coming out of a burning bush—that is a technology that could be easily created by a good ten or fifteen extraterrestrial races. Such a story is an extremely primitive way to get a set of principles to a large group of people. From that story came the teaching of the Ten Commandments, which I honor and respect. It is a very good set of laws to live by. But I think they came from a highly evolved race, which causes me to study the whole question of who and what is "God"? We have been manipulated by extraterrestrial races into believing in a primitive way, whatever the religion we practice, whether Buddhism or Hinduism or Christianity.

Another example is the story of the angel who appeared to Mohammed and dictated the entire religion of Islam. The angel appeared to Mohammed, who was illiterate, but Mohammed was able to recite word for word what the angel said, and that became the written word. Mohammed's ability to recite the angel's message word-for-word, to me, likely happened because the words were repeated internally, in Mohammed's head. This is mental telepathy, which is the way extraterrestrials communicate. I know that if such an ability is available to us today, it had to have been available to us two thousand years ago.

This still does not answer the question of who and what God is. If other races have been involved with our evolution since the beginning, that in itself alters the concept of God. I think our concept of God has been deliberately manipulated to come across in a primitive and palatable way. I think these other races chose to give us a little spoonful of religion as opposed to giving us the concept of God. That may have been done so as not to give humans more than we could handle, and

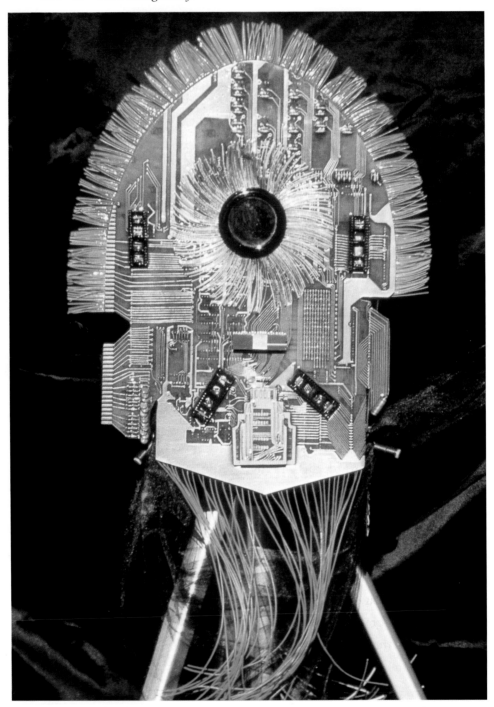

◙ *Metal Headdress*
Marion Martinez, Kiowa

to keep us in check. This gives control to those who manipulate us. I believe that such control is present due to the violent nature of humans. We are, in fact, the single most dangerous species on this planet. We have succeeded in destroying our living resources and ourselves. We now have a technological hold on the planet. We build big machines. We build big guns. We build big bombs. This violence is at the forefront of our existence. The extraterrestrials, whose existence is also possibly threatened, are thereby justified in taking our blood, taking our DNA.

Beyond that there is the duality of benevolent and malevolent interactions. The benevolent races have been the watchers; the malevolent ones have conspired to manipulate us. I feel there has been a war in the heavens, a galactic war. This war has been waged in order to keep us from being polluted and infiltrated by more malevolent species. The solar system, the universe, is filled with the same characteristics that we find on this planet: the ones who have technology and use it for good, and the ones who have technology and use it for their own personal gain no matter who or what they have to destroy.

We now have technology available that can induce a certain kind of vision, one that seems like a dream or a physical experience. You can sit in a lounge chair and put a helmet over your head. Through the helmet a movie is run through your mind. Electrodes are placed on your temples so that you are literally seeing the movie in your brain. A dark screen comes over your eyes and you actually watch the movie with your eyes closed because it is being projected into your mind. So it is more than a movie, more than a three-dimensional event—this is literally a physical experience. You are experiencing the movie through your mental senses, so you can see it, feel it, taste it, smell it.

This holographic technology exists. There are a lot of species who come to Earth and, as part of their recreation, create a vicarious event using humans. They experience vicariously someone else's anger, love, passion, and they feed on that emotion. That is their entertainment.

I don't think it is a lot different in other worlds within the universe than it is in here on our planet. I don't think we get our dangerous side out of nowhere. It comes from somewhere. There is some genetic inheritance. We have some cell memory of being a dominant species, and of being malevolent to the extent that we kill other life-forms and eat them. We do horrible experiments on them.

The fact that we are such a dangerous species means to me that we are not highly evolved. We are growing. Maybe we are a masterpiece in progress; maybe a few of us are closer to becoming masterpieces in progress. I have been given a gift that I treasure. I got my first eagle feather—it is a very sacred gift, very sacred. This comforts me. That is where I want to go, to eagle level. I don't know what it will take to get there, but this is the path for me—the eagle feather will light the way.

I started Stargate International with Robert Dean in 1992. At the time I was working for the city government. I worked with law enforcement agencies and officers dealing with crisis intervention. I was the first resource conservation coordinator for the city of Tucson. I left that job to form Stargate, which came from a dream Robert had. The dream, in essence, conveyed that the stargate will open and the children of the light will return home. This is directly related to the eventual removal of the children of the light from the planet Earth.

The goal of Stargate International is not to be another research organization but to develop educational materials to help people understand what is involved in the paradigm shift. Our goal is to create a resource library so people can seek their own answers. We are primarily oriented toward developing resource materials through videos, slides shows, artwork, lectures—materials for classroom presentation for children in elementary schools. This process of educating people is a wake-up call to realize that we are cornerstones. We can step outside of the pyramid of American society that holds up this infrastructure. If we step outside it can crumble, which it should.

We need a new paradigm on this planet. A paradigm defines the content of a belief system; it creates the borders and boundaries. For example, there is a certain paradigm that the Mexican culture lives inside of—that paradigm is revealed in its traditions, its language, its recipes. Within this paradigm there are certain rules that regulate behavior, so while you are in it you are immersed within its rules. It is very difficult to do something that is strange or not acceptable within the paradigm.

When you have an experience that tells you that your life, within this set of boundaries, could have been impacted by something other than what already lives within this set of boundaries, the paradigm gets turned upside down. Sometimes your paradigm gets infiltrated by someone who comes from a different paradigm. This happens when immigrants come to our country not knowing what is acceptable or not acceptable, what is possible or not possible. They break the "rules" and become successful because no one ever told them that they couldn't do it their particular way.

How is this related to extraterrestrials? We have certain mores that the planet is governed by; we have a certain set of physics that run our planet. The Sun rises in the east, the Sun sets in the west. There is gravity. If you walk off a mountain you fall. If you stand on the ground your feet will always be touching the earth. A certain set of physical "law" forms the paradigm for this planet. Then in comes an extraterrestrial, a craft that hovers. Out come the beings who can levitate, and who can move objects that are extremely heavy. What are they doing? They are breaking the paradigm of our planet, and people are traumatized because their reality of our physical laws is shattered.

The most important fact of a shift such as this is that, if you know this is coming, you can prepare. The Aztecs had a prophecy that said the Spaniards were coming, the "shining ones" were coming. If they had thought ahead the Aztecs would have saved their language, their recipes, their dress—they would have set aside some of their culture so that it would have existed longer in more intact pieces. When one culture comes into an existing culture and the one entering is more technically advanced, everyone in the more primitive culture wants to embrace the new technologies. They will dismiss their own culture to the extent that it is obliterated. The key to a paradigm shift is this: When we are told to hold on to our culture, our language, our ceremonies and songs, the next shift is coming. That is the key. If you want to preserve something of your own origin, preserve it now, because a new technology will come in and that technology will become the dominant culture. The old must be preserved in order not to become obliterated, erased, forgotten. Otherwise it will fade away. That is the most important reason for preparing for this shift.

Preparation for the shift is the most intensive research I have done for Stargate International. A culture that loses its reality as embedded in traditional physics is an entire culture in crisis, a paradigm crisis. All of a sudden everything that we have known about physics will not apply anymore. Everything we have known about time will not apply anymore. Everything we have known about space and gravity will not apply anymore. Nor will our knowledge of God or religion.

Most of the extraterrestrials we come into contact with are on military programs. The ones who are traveling space are generally either on a scientific mission or a military mission. They are not civilians from another planet. These vessels are on reconnaissance, which is why their inhabitants wear uniforms and insignias. That is why, when people make reports of craft landings, they say this one was wearing this insignia or this uniform. Reports that I know well say the Blondes or the Nordics all wear uniforms. If you think of how our military operates, this is logical.

In some cases angels and extraterrestrials are indistinguishable, depending on the race. They may look angelic to us, but that is according to our paradigm, not theirs. We have been taught that certain physical characteristics are those of an angel. People who appear in front of human beings, like Gabriel or Mary or Jesus or Mohammed, are said to look like this. This is an angel to us, but maybe they just got beamed down.

Right now the common belief by military personnel is that there are well over one hundred races. In 1947 the military knew of twelve races. In the mid-1950s and '60s that number rose to fifty or sixty. Today it's well over one hundred. The Star Katsinas are among the most ancient.

It is commonly believed that the Nordics, the angelic-looking ones, are the ones who created the Greys. The Greys are a biological entity created in a laboratory. This is called genetic engineering.

The beliefs are so varied and there are so many of them that it is really difficult to figure out what is true and what is not. Who is benevolent and who isn't? Who is acting out of evolutionary purpose and who is acting out of personal gain and control? Who is in charge of our planet? It certainly isn't human beings. Who is monitoring whom? I do believe we are at a crucial turning point for our solar system, and maybe for a larger arena. This is the watering hole. Inside the planet there is also extraterrestrial activity.

When I was working for the county attorney's office I did crisis intervention; my job was called "victim-witness advocate." I was on a pager and often on call at home. My team responded to bank robberies, drive-by shootings, kidnappings, and other incidents of violence. We knew the code and protocol of national victims organizations; we took the Mitchell protocols dealing with posttraumatic stress disorder. We also learned critical-incident stress debriefing. The protocols were different relative to whether the incident involved an individual or a group. I took a lot of training over the years to be effective in that job.

At one point I began going into the field with Robert Dean to investigate various UFO sites and case files. All the particulars were taken into account: What time? What color? How much? When? Where did you go? What was the date? What was the hour? What did it look like? These were the MUFON (Mutual UFO Network) protocols from the manual for training investigators. When I went on these field inquiries Robert would deal with the individuals who had a sighting and ask all these questions. I asked all the crisis questions: How are you feeling? Where are you staying tonight? Are you alone?

As time went on it became clear that my questions were of great help to the witnesses of UFOs. Eventually this became a most valuable

■ *Sky Deity*
Cliff Fragua, Jemez Pueblo

tool for dealing with the investigation, and I created a three-day training program to teach people to do crisis intervention for contactees
and abductees. I established a training manual and put on the first
training seminar with thirty-three graduates from different communities across the country. Out of that class seven people came together
in Tucson and formed the first hotline for people who wanted to
get counseling over their abductions—what they had seen or felt or

dreamed. We have hundreds of statistical cases at Stargate since the hotline's inception.

There is a tremendously wide range of experiences. The Bigelow Report (created by Robert Bigelow from the Bigelow Foundation in Las Vegas, Nevada), is another statistical study, this one from a nationwide poll conducted by the Roper organization to record the incidents of extraterrestrial contact. All the statistics have been published. This is a positive step toward more widespread acceptance of UFO experiences. The report supported the training I conducted, in which people were taught how to set up a hotline with the idea that they would go back to their communities and train others on the hotline protocols. Let's take, for example, the incident in Phoenix known as "the Phoenix lights." Many, many people witnessed this craft, nearly a mile in width. A city councilwoman, Francis Barwood, made a statement to the people of Phoenix after her phone was flooded with distress calls. Those calls were able to be directed to a team of professionals, supporting the public (and the councilwoman) in dealing with the experience. This is a perfect example of how a hotline works.

Right now there is a great deal of controversy about how advanced our technology is. There is speculation that we, in fact, have rendered craft similar to those from other realms. Area 51 in Nevada (also called "Dreamland"), site of the world's most secret military tests, is also the location of the U.S. government's top-secret UFO research program. Insiders claim that recovered spacecraft from an extraterrestrial civilization are back-engineered and test flown there. Indeed, over the years hundreds of witnesses have observed strange maneuvers of disc-shaped craft over the "black world" of Groom Lake. In a three-year investigation a German film crew dove deeply into the secrets of Dreamland, interviewing top scientists and security personnel who worked inside Area 51 and claim to have seen the recovered craft and even alien lifeforms—"guests" of the U.S. government. They captured on film the remarkable maneuvers of these mysterious UFOs. The film documentation also includes detailed interviews with nuclear physicist Robert

Lazar regarding his work at Nellis Airforce Base, and footage of strange craft and their maneuvers over that site.

If you look at the publicity surrounding the extraterrestrial phenomena in the press, on TV, in Hollywood you will find a particularly malevolent portrait. I don't think this is coincidental. The U.S. military may go so far as to stage UFO activity and then ask Congress to appropriate more weapons. The military survives by contracting to build more weapons, so the government must maintain a wartime economy at all cost. Regardless, there is going to be a mass return of the true extraterrestrial confederation. Look at the sightings in Mexico City, the largest city in the world. The sightings are phenomenal. We get reports all the time from Mexico.

People have a variety of experiences with extraterrestrials. Some are called abductions, and that's exactly what they are. Other people are contactees, and they are very comfortable with their experiences. Some people are treated with dignity and respect, thereby giving the individual a lot of flexibility in how they want to react to the experience. Other people are not given any choices whatsoever—they are simply taken and experimented with. They have had their sperm or their eggs stolen. From our research it seems that there are many groups visiting Earth now. Some come to perform sociological experiments, others to run geological experiments on the planet, and others come to get water. This is called the Blue Star planet, the watering hole. Each group has a different reason for coming. How the people who live here respond to these visitors, how humans react, depends entirely on each individual's experience.

People who have biological experiments performed on them are extremely traumatized. There are a number of women we have talked to through Stargate who have simply been used as incubators. The women never take a child to full-term delivery; they incubate a fetus for up to three or four or five months and then the pregnancies are taken from them. The reports indicate that the women are pregnant one day and not pregnant the next. Some women, being treated for their pregnancy in the first trimester, have doctor's records. All of a sudden the pregnancy has disappeared. There is no miscarriage, no abortion—the fetus is simply there one day, and then it is not there. Some women get abducted at night in their sleep and have the fetus taken from them. Conversely, women who have been barren for years get pregnant. The technology is so advanced that pregnancy is possible.

Sometimes the recall of such an experience comes a long time after the actual event. Again, each incident creates different reactions, different fears. But recognizing the paradigm shift is essential. We discovered that if you can explain to someone that what they are experiencing—the fear, the trauma—is due to the fact that their way of understanding life around them has changed, then you can help them recover. Helping them to understand why they are in trauma can speed the recovery.

I received a call once from a woman in Chandler, Arizona, who said she woke up one morning and could not stop crying for remembering a dream she had. This dream scared her deeply. She dreamed that she was on a clinical table, in an office, and that she had an instrument inserted into her rectum. What scared her was not that she had the dream, but that when she awoke there was blood coming from her rectum. (Rectal exams are a common experience reported by abductees.) I spoke at length with the woman several times and used all the crisis intervention tools in my repertoire to support her.

The questions people ask the most are who? and why? At Stargate we have a bank of cases that shed light on these questions, and bring the information to a more palatable level. When the woman from Chandler called I was able to tell her that the equipment she reported as having been used on her had been reported before. This was a comfort to her. We assist people in that way.

One of our projects is a congressional initiative. The purpose of this project is to provide a positive means through which the reality of extraterrestrial contact can be made known to the American public. The project seeks to do this educating in a serious and informative manner, thereby minimizing the shock, negative sensationalism, and potentially chaotic response to the information. The challenges this issue presents necessitate a formal and focused political strategy. We have therefore chosen to embark on a path to resolve the existing gap between fact and cover-up. Our political structure provides for the direct petitioning of our elected officials while protecting the petitioners. Therefore the initiative proposes an action plan designed to create a realistic and practical framework of support for direct political action by our senators and representatives. We will pursue the path of a congressional hearing for view by all Americans.

What may well be the most significant information in our history lies buried in archives while our children grow up in ignorance and fear. Stargate stands for a single principle: full and complete disclosure of all UFO material. The purpose is to challenge Congress to conduct open hearings on the release of classified documents related to UFOs and extraterrestrial contact that meet the thirty- and fifty-year rule. The time has come to let humanity know the truth. Extraterrestrial intelligence is present on planet Earth. What does this mean? And where do we, as the human race, go from here? The people of the planet Earth are looking into the eyes of a new millennium. Are we prepared? There is proof of an age-old interrelationship between the human race and advanced extraterrestrial intelligence. This presence on our planet has existed for at least the last thirty thousand years. Many researchers believe that open and worldwide contact with ETs is just around the corner. This may be the most exciting time to be alive on the planet Earth.

We also created a survival kit. I do believe that the Earth changes that are coming are going to be great. I believe that after the year 2000 we will be moving very quickly toward this occurrence. Somewhere between the year 2000 and 2012 we will be in the eye of the Earth changes. Some of it has already begun. We are already having a lot of earthquakes, some volcanic eruptions, tornadoes, and floods of significant size. All of these will escalate considerably. The time between events gets smaller and smaller. I tell people at every conference I attend to be sure to have a survival kit in either your car or your home, or both. This includes a flashlight, flashlight batteries, candles, matches, extra

jackets, blankets, a pillow. Make sure you have extra canned goods in your pantry. I would say to have at least a week's worth of food—more if you can. Store canned foods, dried foods, powdered foods that you can rehydrate. Store absolutely enough water to survive on for a week and, if it is at all possible, get something with which you can purify water. We are going to be affected through the disruption of the transportation system. Food will not arrive at the grocery store on time. The trucks that carry food back and forth will not be able to get through. Highways will be going out from floods or earthquakes.

If the network out of Los Angeles gets disrupted, like it happened in San Francisco, you can forget getting produce. Oklahoma, Utah, all the central states will receive nothing from the coasts. Earth's upheavals will disrupt produce from getting through at all. If we have any earthquakes in the vicinity of nuclear power plants the electricity will go down in the cities, so you will need candles, hurricane lanterns, kerosene lanterns. I hope to have a small generator soon. You can use this to keep a small refrigerator going. If you have a baby, if you have children, you want milk in the refrigerator. You want to keep some things cold—that will take a generator. The only drawback is that for a generator you need gasoline, which you can't store because it goes bad. You can get a generator that runs on diesel fuel, which you can store.

As far as heat goes, invest in a woodstove and store cords of wood in your backyard. One should take as many survival precautions as can be thought of. Have extra blankets on hand, a first-aid kit, a bicycle or a horse—any alternate transportation. If you have the opportunity to establish a root cellar, do so. Make a garden, plant herbs, put up canned foods of any kind. In the root cellar you should have as much food as would feed your whole family—not just family that lives with you, but also family nearby. In my case, for example, I have two sisters and three brothers. None of them live in an area where they would have a root cellar. So whichever one has the opportunity to dig a root cellar, build it for all the family. Learning how to grow your own food and herbs is what will be required. Have a small greenhouse anywhere on your property. All of that is what I do now.

Wherever you have a particular kind of weather, say in Arizona, where I live, it will be exaggerated. It will become hotter. Wherever it is cold it will become colder. The climates will continue to change. It's preparation time now and we have very little time left. No one knows for sure when, but we are in the changes now.

The extraterrestrials were here before us. They came to the planet a long time before us. They were most likely visiting this planet when it was inhabited by dinosaurs, and they have been coming to and leaving this planet for a long time. We were created as part of their force,

■ *Ziggurat*
Oscar Rodriguez, Tarahumara

and in creating us they included in our DNA a lot of handicaps, propensities for illness, for maladies. If they had done a thorough job they would have taken the genetic problems out of the DNA. Good geneticists today create "perfect" products, like cloned sheep. If they are ready to announce that they have cloned sheep, you can bet they have cloned lots of other species. I believe they have cloned humans. There is no way they would announce cloning sheep, having perfected that process, without having gone way beyond that phase already.

We are indeed a hybrid species on the planet. We have been influenced genetically by the various groups that have come to this planet. The five root races—White, Black, Yellow, Red, Brown—have likely been influenced by five different extraterrestrial species. Remember, Genesis says, "We were created in their image." *Their* is plural. *Elohim,* from Genesis in the Bible, is plural. We were created in their image. The five root races were influenced by different injections of DNA. When we get reports that some of the extraterrestrials look like us, the truth is that we look like them. We are indeed their children, and some of them come back to look after their own, to see how we're evolving. They have a scientific interest in us.

Any good geneticist will follow whatever it is he is creating. Just like a good scientist today will tag a tiger, a bear, a whale, we are also tagged. The implants people report receiving are so that the extraterrestrials can find us again, or at least find the ones they are interested in. The geneticists—the extraterrestrials—can reproduce another you by taking out your DNA. They can clone you at will by taking a piece of you. We have been allowed to evolve and have a life here. That doesn't mean that the extraterrestrials don't still need us. They do, to mind the planet.

The extraterrestrial craft used the ancient sites as recharging zones, like a great battery. They used the ancient monuments, the pyramids and the ziggurat, the edifice with steps coming up to a flat surface. You will see these monuments in Central and South America, in Mexico, in Egypt, and even in the United States. All of these were built using a workforce—not manually, but using technology. Human beings were always created as the caretakers. In the jungles today in South America and Mexico there still exist many active landing sites. The pyramids are like the hangar where you store craft. The ziggurats are the landing spots.

If the Master Teachers are the ones who, for genetic reasons, care for us, then I will say this may not be true for all extraterrestrial species. There are those who are not concerned at all with our evolution. And there are those who are in touch with indigenous people. I accept their concern for the planet at this time. Those teachings should benefit all of humankind, or we will not evolve.

WE ARE ALL STAR SEED

The ancient ones   Whether technological   Or spiritual   Are entering
into   Our paradigm shift   Changing the geography   Of our Blue Star
We call home   Root races   We call human   A time   We call now

We are   All star seed   Born again spirits   Of many dimensions   Seen
and unseen   Heard and unheard   Known and unknown

The true nature   Of our reality   The great mystery   Of time and space
Encounters   A secret presence   A reunion   Embraced   Transformed
Into the worlds   Above and beyond

Paradigm shift   Preparations   Saving the language   Saving the recipes
Saving the ceremonies   Honoring the cultures   Of our origin   Opening
the stargate

Hold the earth   Within your hands   Interwoven flesh with soil   Work as
one   Becomes whole   Moisture saturating   Turning the soil   Waxing
and waning   With the moon   Share the earth   Harvest for all   Merge
For a higher purpose

Smell the fragrance   From birth to death   A vessel shape   Shifting
into matter   Aromatic passion of cell by cell   Moving into sacred
geometry   Shapes of continuum   Ever-changing shapes of mind   A
light force   Within her garden   Scented medicine of breath   The
colors of the powers   All Mother

10 WE DO NOT TAKE OUR TAKE OUR BODIES WITH US

Developing Psychic Powers

SHONA BEAR CLARK

Stay together always. You will also live at the highest point of my pyramid. Each of you will be a Star. Take care of the Light I leave within my temple.

GREAT MAYAN LAW OF HUNAB'KU

My first craft sighting was in 1970 in Roxbury, Connecticut, when I was twenty years old and attending the New School of Social Research in New York City. I saw lights through the skylight in my apartment, and was told to travel out of the city to an isolated location in the country. I brought a friend along to witness what would happen.

I was summoned intuitively to the middle of a field. A triangular formation maneuvered on the horizon. Then one craft came forward and its light disappeared. The craft proceeded to directly where I was standing; it hovered some two hundred feet above my head. A field of energy transmitted information to me.

I was told that I had work to do pertaining to them. Although I believe there were no living beings in that craft, I felt the ships had been sent from a larger vehicle. At no time did I feel threatened or afraid. Instead there was a tremendous sense of well-being, and confirmation of a more highly advanced technology and presence. I knew that we were not alone.

Finding my cousin Shona Bear, a powerful Indian doctor, is one of the greatest gifts of my journey. Our lives are now connected forever. She has been teaching me the old ways of the "Five Civilized People"—Cherokee, Creek, Seminole, Choctaw, and Chickasaw—and through her I have begun to learn prayers in sign language.

The Star Ancestors have announced themselves to me and provided my instructions—this is my walkabout, my vision quest. Collecting the teachings will continue as my primary work. We are standing in the great change of cycles. The ancestors stand among us. —NRS

Shona Bear Clark was born of the Wind Clan and raised on the Creek Indian reservation near Oklahoma City. Tall and light-skinned with high cheekbones and fine features, Shona Bear descends from a proud line of medicine women. Immersed since childhood in secret knowledge and fluent in the sign language of the Creek, Shona is a practitioner of ritualistic healing arts. My cousin on my mother's side, she is the mother of seven, grandmother of seventeen, and great-grandmother of one. We speak during a cold March day in Shona's adobe artist's studio in Santa Fe, New Mexico.

Lydia Tiger, "Ladiga" in Creek, was a well-known and very powerful Indian doctor. She was the grandmother of Alex Posey, the famous Creek poet. Lydia was my great-great-grandmother. She lived to be a hundred and fifteen. Lydia was a healer. Often she would have spirits coming to her. She would sprinkle tobacco around the house, not always wanting to communicate with them. This is where my mother got her training, and I, in turn, got mine.

My mother is eighty-four years old. She's always used telepathy to communicate with her children. When my mother wants me to call home, it's like somebody hits me with a hammer on the head until I call. When I get in touch she always asks, "What took you so long?" I used telepathy as a young mother to communicate with my children. My kids could be out in the yard and I'd be sitting inside and feeling a great need for a hug. One time I thought about my three-year-old daughter and visualized her coming in, and within fifteen minutes she came inside. She came in, looking almost hypnotized, then got on my lap and hugged me. My mother, who was sitting next to me, slapped me on the leg and said, "Stop doing that. I know what you're doing." For some reason she did not want me to use telepathy at will.

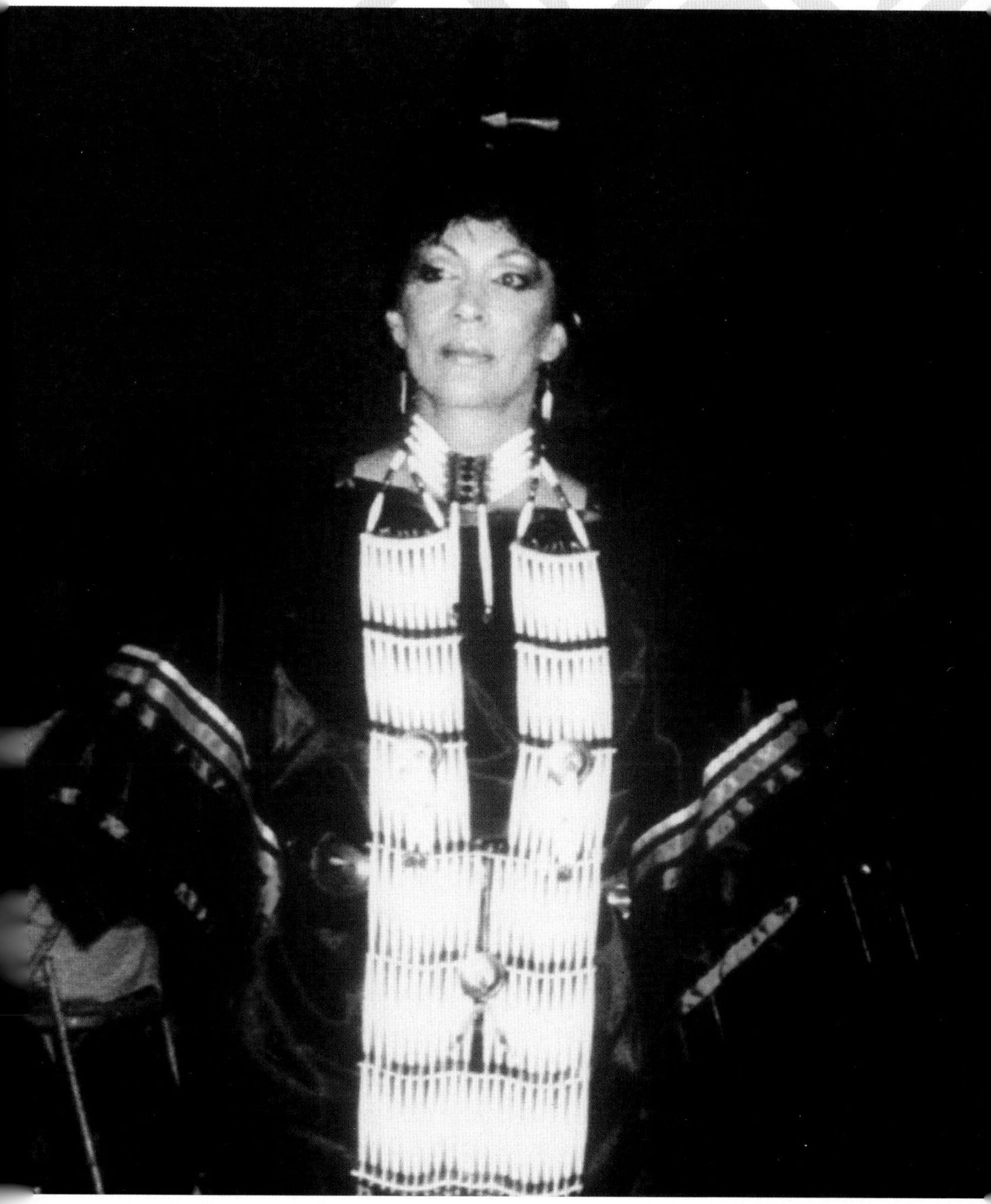

Shona Bear Clark
Creek Nation, Oklahoma

People think that we are individuals, not connected, but in my experience it's different. If you have a thought, somebody else has it too; if you put a thought out there somebody is going to pick it up. For every action there is another action, and for every thought there is also another thought.

People pick up on your thoughts, and they don't have to be in the room with you. My nephew was shot in the head; the bullet entered the right ear, traveled around the base of the skull, and lodged behind the left ear. The doctors said that he would be in coma for at least five days; they really didn't know if he would ever come out of it. My family asked if I could do anything for my nephew. I told them I would try.

I lay down and went into the base of my skull, as I've been trained to do. There is a little indentation at the base of the skull. You bring medicine out from that point. You bring that medicine down to your left hand—when your left hand becomes tingly you know that you are ready to work. So I drew the medicine from the base of my skull, and when my hand started to vibrate with sensation I left my body. My nephew was two hundred and fifty miles away. I went into his head with my finger. I followed the tracks of the wound to his left ear, where I found a dark, dark spot. I tried to dig that out but I couldn't get it. It wasn't the bullet I felt; there was something black in there. That moment the phone rang and I was told my nephew had regained consciousness. I was still dazed from the trance I was in. After I hung up the phone he slipped back into coma. His mother called and asked me if I could go back in.

I waited about four hours. It was evening then, and very quiet. When I went back in again I found the black spot, but there was no way to get it out. During this second intervention my nephew again regained consciousness for fifteen or twenty minutes. I told his mother that there was something in there I couldn't get out. He went back into coma and stayed that way for four days. Then he came to. When he awoke he said that there had been a witch in his room.

The bullet had damaged the brain. He has no long-term or even short-term memory. That was the black spot. That was how my mother explained it to me.

I'm not a doctor. I know nothing about the brain. I work with medicine, but I'm not an M.D. I was taught that the base of the skull is where you go when you need to do medicine. This makes your hand like an X-ray machine with which you can feel things in people's bodies. You pull all your energy out from the base of the brain and it goes into your left hand. This is why your hand tingles.

My mother started teaching me by drawing circles on my hand, with her hand, from a six-inch distance. Then she would draw squares, then crosses, so I could feel them. She would pull her hand farther back, continuing to concentrate on my hand until I felt what she was drawing.

Then you are there. You can feel the circle. You can move this energy. You have to draw the energy from the base of the skull, where your head sits on your neck. This is the place of the brain stem. My mother taught me that a little farther up in there is a house. This house sits inside the middle of the brain. This little house is what you clean when you become confused or disturbed. You go in there mentally and wash the house. You unplug the things that are bothering you. One side of the house has a black wall where the plugs are, and there are sockets, which you can disconnect. You must keep this house very clean and peaceful because it is the center of your being.

You can go there as a place of refuge or you can go there to make contact in other dimensions, to travel the universe. You create a quiet zone, and then you focus between your eyes, right into the middle of your forehead. You look, but your eyes are closed. You see a haze, like a purple mist with a little bit of white to it. Then you will find a small hole. You go through that hole and come to a tiny hole, a much smaller one, and you've got to slip through that. Once there, anything is possible. It's a matter of centering yourself. You can stay there as long as you want. So when I have a need I go inside that little room, project myself out, and travel. Every time I have left my body I have looked back and seen my body. I never once took my body with me on any trip.

□ *Feather Dancer*
Shona Bear Clark, Creek

The first step is to learn to be alone. You have to know how to be alone. You have to learn to make yourself quiet. You have to be still. You have to be able to look inside yourself and clear your vision, not think or receive thoughts. Most people cannot sit still and be alone. They are not self-entertained.

In order to travel we have to purify ourselves. If one is not a garbage collector one's body does not become the city dump. I take care of my body, and I take care of my house. To do this I make my own holy water. Indians don't call it holy water, but we put sage and tobacco, Indian tobacco, into a little bit of water. I recently got tobacco up at Onondaga, Six Nations—ceremonial tobacco for women who no longer have their Moon. It's Indian grown and beautiful; it almost smells like apricots.

First you breathe into the water, you blow into it. Then you blow into the tobacco and sage, mindfully. I put the tobacco and sage into a small bag—that way I can concentrate on the breath. You're breathing the life of Creator; you go into a different state of mind. Then I pour the tobacco and sage into the water and let it sit for twenty-four hours. After twenty-four hours you go through each room and sprinkle the water at the doorways and the windows, and on everything in the house that you feel needs purification. Then you smoke your house with sage, cedar, or both. The smoke comes through the house and picks up all the negative debris. As you smoke the house you open the doors and the windows, and you take the smoke to the doors and windows and ask the entities or spirits that are present to leave, to leave with love. You tell them they are not wanted. Then you draw a circle in the center of the house—I sometimes do this with sand—and leave the water bowl there for the night. The water sucks everything negative into the bowl. Then you take the bowl outside. You dig a hole and bury the bowl, pouring the water out into the hole.

My training in telepathy started as a little girl, with my mother talking to me in my room. I have never forgotten anything she said. I can quote poetry for hours because that's what she did. Her uncle, Alex Posey, was a famous poet, so she quoted poetry constantly. She talked poetry inside her head, and I heard it.

From the time I was a little girl my mother taught me to protect myself by dropping a cone-shaped shield over my body. You do this four times. Each shield is made of precious substances—like pearl, gold, silver, platinum, or precious stones or shells. The cone shield protects you from psychic debris, so you don't pick up on other people's garbage or allow anybody else to dump any garbage on you. You can drop that cone over your home in the same manner. I do this every night for myself and for my children—for everyone I know and love. I drop such a cone over their houses to protect them. Any time I feel sorry for myself, when I am beside myself with my own problems, I lie down and I pray for fifty people by name and I drop cones of protection over them. That's the only way I can stop wallowing in my own self-pity and sorrow. Sending people good energy is a way to engage in a more helpful manner. I try to focus on their hearts, because we live and we center in the heart, and in the pit of our stomachs. If you press four fingers into the solar plexus, that will free your energy. I was taught that as a little girl.

Sometimes I lie down and place a round stone on my belly. The stone has to be fairly heavy. The stone becomes a focus point. I was taught that when things are in your body that don't belong there, the way to pull them out is to place a stone on that place, near your pelvic bone. You have to visualize these energies going out of your body through the stone. You see the energy as color—gray-blue or green or whatever color it might be to you. You see it coming out of your body into the stone and then back into the earth. The stone acts as a magnet. When I was sick as a child I was always sick in colors. The color I saw would tell where the illness was.

Another person who taught me a lot is Sonny, Will Sampson. Most people know him as an actor, but he was a painter too. When I was a

◻ *Cherokee Mask*
Jim Farris, Cherokee

young woman he would take me up the hill to walk across stones as big as houses. He told me that to find the Creator you had to go into the mountains and into yourself, to be quiet and still and not have thoughts of your own. Suddenly Spirit will appear to you.

My father was a very powerful man. He was half Cherokee and half German. His mother, a full-blooded Cherokee, was related to Will Rogers; also, some say, to Bonnie Parker. That's how we are related—my father was a Parker and your mother is a Parker. Most people don't realize that Bonnie Parker of Bonnie and Clyde was a Cherokee.

My grandfather did not speak English; all he spoke was German and Cherokee. My grandmother spoke Cherokee. She tried to be like a White lady, but she looked completely Indian and she had Indian ways. She wanted to be White but she still lived by the traditional ways.

When I was a little girl, when a storm came my father would sharpen a double-edged ax and stand at the corners of the house. He would turn that ax in the four directions to cut the storm. He would just cut it loose from the house, then sprinkle tobacco around the house. The storms would never come near our house. We have a lot of tornadoes in Oklahoma, but not at our house.

He practiced a lot of traditional ways, Indian ways. People would come from all over to ask him for crop predictions. He would see their crops in dreams and visions and he would tell them what to plant. He was never wrong, so the farmers and people who planted came from all over to ask what type of crops they should have that year. My father was very psychic. He knew things and he could work with that knowledge. He would bring objects to himself: a tool, or whatever else he needed. My father would materialize things in his hand, but he told me when you do something like that you can never keep it. You could look at it, turn it over, but never use it. If you did, he said, it would disappear in your hand. What he manifested came from a place that required those things be returned. My father could also make dice flip over and fall into a seven. He was not a gambler, but in times of hardship or serious need he would shoot dice. And he never lost because he made the dice turn. Because of this he was frightened, so he never did much gambling—only if we really needed the money to feed the family.

Being a lot like him, my father and I spent a lot of time together. He was an Indian doctor. He removed cancers and warts from people. He would take a piece of cedar and make something that looked like a knife. He would rub it across the cancer or warts, and the next day they would be gone. He took a cancer the size of my thumbnail off a woman's nose once. When he took it out it had legs like a spider, like a daddy longlegs. It left a big hole in her nose, and he pulled it together and taped the hole up. I saw him remove moles off people's heads, moles that looked like strawberries. He removed his own cancer; the doctor said he'd never seen a cleaner removal of a cancer in his life. My father wouldn't give the instructions to anybody. He said that in the hands of the wrong people it wouldn't be good. If somebody used the information in a wrong way, it would be deadly.

My father was a storyteller and a man of great humor. He was a fiddler. He made his own fiddle out of a tree. He rode broncos and rode them well. He had long red hair that went past his waist, chestnut colored. He looked like he was on fire. He was a masculine man; every part of his body was a muscle. He could lift a thousand pounds to his knees. People came from miles by covered wagon to see him wrestle because he'd wrestle two men at once. I never met a kinder, more gentle man. Everybody loved him. He was well respected, a man of his word. Men have lost the ability to be good for their word. He never talked about people. He didn't run them down. If he didn't like someone they knew it. He would go directly to them. He'd give you the shirt off his back, but if you crossed him you'd be sorry. He killed a man when he was twelve years old. He shot a man over a legal debt. In those days that was the way it was.

My father was eighty-four when he died. A piece of me died that day. The day he died the house was filled with people. It was winter but there were so many people in the house it was hot, like a summer day. I never knew a human being that did not like my father, so many,

□ *Coming From The Dark*
Shona Bear Clark, Creek

many people were there—men and women and children. The night he died I was standing in the living room where my father's body was lying. All of a sudden a man came down the hallway. He was a young man, about twenty-three years old. He had on a western shirt, a new pair of Levi's, and fine boots, and he had red hair. He just strutted down that hallway, his shoulders back. He walked into the living room, looked at everybody, turned around, and walked out the door. I followed him. He walked straight to the turnpike and just disappeared. I knew it was my father. I recognized him, walking proud, straight and big. He disappeared in front of my eyes.

I went back into the house and my mother asked, "Who was that young man?" Later in the bedroom she asked me again. I told her, "You know who it was. He came into the living room, walked on that hard floor, and his feet never once touched the ground. It was Dad." The floors in that house were wood, hard wood. You couldn't walk in there without making a sound. My mother said she noticed that too. It got to where everybody was asking who that man was. They, too, noticed his feet never touched the floor. I didn't tell anybody the truth, and I don't think my mother did either.

My daddy once told me about his dog that came back. It was dead—he'd seen the bones of it—but it came back to the house. My father tried to feed it but it wouldn't eat. It stayed at his house four days, jumped and played, ran around and barked. But it never left a track; its feet never touched the ground. My father said that animals had spirits and people had spirits, and spirits never walked on the earth.

One day, when my father had been dead over a year, the phone rang. It was summertime. I picked up the phone and heard my father ask, "Honey, are you all right?" It threw me into such shock. I said, "Daddy, Daddy, is that you?" He laughed and asked again, "Are you all right, honey?" Then the phone went dead. I was beside myself. I jumped up and ran into the living room. Then the doorbell rang and the hair on the back of my neck stood up. I was scared to death. Suddenly the alarm on my truck went off, there were police outside, and someone was running by the house. A gun went off. I became totally petrified.

The police came to the door. There had been a murder and the man they were chasing had run by my bedroom window when the phone rang. That phone call saved my life.

When I was a little girl I had scarlet fever. I was kept in a darkened room for several years. My mother was told that I could go blind if I was exposed to sunlight. During this time little white children with blonde hair would come into my room at night, right through the walls, and play with me. They would take me out of my body.

Then, when I was seven, one of these beings saved my life. My mother had left the house. I was playing outside in the yard. A man came by on a horse and asked if I wanted a ride. Naturally I said yes. I rode on his lap a few miles from the house. He stopped the horse, took me down, hit me on the head with a rock, and left me bloody on the ground. Then a blonde man with blue eyes came. He had on a shiny silver jumpsuit with half-inch yellow stripes down the sides. He stopped my head from bleeding and carried me within ten steps of my house. Then he put me down and said, "Go to your mama." I tried to do as he said. I called her but passed out in the yard. I spent two weeks in the hospital. I didn't see the Blondes again for many years.

One evening, after the incident and the hospitalization, I was home on the reservation again. I was looking out the window to the creek. We have an arbor there. The snow was heavy. I heard someone calling from the arbor, "Come on, Shona Bear. Come on." I thought it was my mother calling me. But when I went to the door I could see them—tall figures with black robes and black hoods, coaxing me forward. Later my mama said, "Don't ever go when they call. They can't have you unless you go to them." My mother told me she'd seen them—the ones in the black robes. She called them blood-head people, angels of death.

As a young woman of twenty I died from uncontrolled bleeding during childbirth. Because I have O-negative blood, a donor was difficult to find. As the blood drained out of me I shot out of my body. I was on the ceiling, surrounded by a warm light of pure love. I saw all that I'd always seen and what I had only vaguely glimpsed. There was nothing I didn't completely understand. I knew the secrets of the universe.

Then I felt an odd sensation. I became aware that someone was tying a tag and someone else was saying the Lord's Prayer. I was looking down on them from above. Then suddenly I was back in my body. I felt like I was breathing through clay; I wasn't getting enough air. I had been dead for seven minutes. I was in pure light. I didn't see or hear anyone in the light, but ever since then I have been able to hear people thinking. I can see a person's spirit floating above his head, which tells me a great deal about the person.

I didn't see a spacecraft until I was twenty-five and my small daughter had been badly bitten by a dog. We set off in a couple of cars, myself and my closest family and friends, driving to the hospital as fast as we could. On the way a saucer-shaped object came down from the sky and hovered a short distance above us. It was silver and looked like two saucers, one over the other, with a line around the middle made of windows. We pulled over and got out of the car. There must have been ten of us. Above us we could see figures in the windows. Everyone got scared except my daughter and me. They all got back in the cars and were yelling for us to come too, but we had left our bodies and entered the craft. The Blonde men I knew from earlier in my life were there, enveloped in a pale blue light. They examined my injured girl, and either cured her or determined that she was not in danger. Then the saucer rose up and disappeared, as if through a hole in the sky. When I looked down from the hole my daughter and I were on the ground again, staring at each other in amazement. Everyone else had driven off. The next night that craft came back and stayed over my mother's house for nearly two hours. We weren't afraid.

When I saw the UFO with my daughter we went on the ship. They did something to my daughter. We did not take our bodies with us. Bodies are nothing. They don't mean anything.

There is no difference between the Blonde beings and what people call angels. I didn't see one of the Blondes again until I was forty-three. It had been a cold winter and my father had pneumonia. On my way to check on him one day I encountered a white man standing in the front yard of my father's house. I thought he was a preacher. He had blue eyes and shoulder-length hair. He was wearing a light-blue suit, what seemed to be a clergyman's collar, and black patent leather shoes. I passed within three feet of him, paused, and then asked him who he was. He just smiled and said, "Everything is going to be fine." Then I blinked and he was gone. Inside, my father was greatly recovered. He was in the kitchen making coffee. I asked my mother who the white man was and she looked out the window and stared at me funny. I told my father about what had happened and he just laughed and said, "Maybe it was my guardian angel." I went back outside to look for him again, but there weren't any tracks in the snow.

Lately I know most things before they happen. And much to my surprise, my telepathy is increasing. I'm spending much time alone. Within my circle of intimates I can speak sign language, and so I can extend the periods of silence. I'm painting tepee designs on hides. The designs are pyramids also. There is much dancing and ceremony. I hadn't planned on this, but things are proceeding more quickly than the world wants to admit. It happens suddenly, and you're in it.

Like last summer—it was late July. I woke up suddenly in the night. It was 3:32 a.m., according to my clock. My room was completely lit up but the lamp wasn't on. At first I thought the light was coming from outside, but then I realized it wasn't. I looked down at my foot—there was a piece missing, about one-inch deep and three-inches long. The inside of my foot looked silver, but there was no blood. All at once I became aware of two men standing next to me, one on each side. Their bodies were passing through the bed. They had blonde shoulder-length hair and blue eyes and looked to be about fifty years old. Their skin was a bronze color, as if they were tanned. They wore robes. One robe was red and white with gold roping around the collar, and the other was blue and white with gold roping. The man in the blue robe passed his hand over my foot and said, "Shona, you are completely healed." The other man put his hands on each side of my head without touching me and said, "We will be back when you need us."

When they disappeared my foot looked normal, but the light remained until around six in the morning. The whole time I felt as if I were bathed in love. They healed my foot. They have great power, and I feel they want me to know they gave me this power. When I was born, they were there. They have always been here. They are here to help. They don't live here, but in another place. They told me to paint hides. They wanted hummingbirds, deer, and pyramids—full diamonds and half diamonds. The pyramid is now the predominant shape in my work.

So few Earth people understand what is happening. Earth is being destroyed, and the people will go with it. I try to wake them up. What else is there to do at this time?

Three weeks ago I woke up at 11:30 p.m. to find a man standing in my room. He had blonde hair to his shoulders and blue eyes and was wearing a white robe with gold roping around the neck. He said, "We are giving you back your memories." That's all he said. He stood there all night as I slept on and off. After that I began leaving my body again regularly. Many times I've spoken to spirits and they've taken me out of my body and guided me places. I have lived a long life, continually aware of the existence of other realities and of strange, magical beings who can traverse the dimensional barriers and enter my world. These are things Indians rarely speak about to White men. But we are changing all that now.

When I got my memories back I saw their world. I saw their home. They let me visit. I saw a world that had three suns, and the land looked orange. It was sandy. I saw Earth; there were seven rings around it. The Blondes live in one of those rings, one of those realms. They interact with humans, but they aren't angels. They are a race of beings who would not go against the Creator and the original instructions. They would prefer death than to go against the Creator, who allowed them to stay there. They interact with humans, trying to help humans, to save them. Human beings are so fragile and so self-destructive at the same time. I've painted these Blonde people; my children have seen them. They dress completely in white, and sometimes they have children with them.

One time I locked both sets of keys inside my truck. I could see the keys inside. My son told me he could break in through the window. I decided not to do that and went inside to think a minute. Then I said, "Well, if you're here, help me find the keys." I said it out of anger to the beings who had so often visited me. All of a sudden something took my hand and dragged me to the back of the house, to my bedroom. My son was watching. There was a little basket sitting on my dresser and there was a white stone in it, about palm size. I still have the stone. My hand was thrust into the basket, and when I brought it out the stone was in my hand. Under the stone was one key, which opened the door to my truck. My son asked me why I had put the key there. I told him I hadn't—the keys were in the truck. When we opened the truck the key that let us in was missing from the key ring. I know now that I am heavily protected.

I've seen things and lately I can feel them. I know that the time is closer and closer. Other people tell me that they know something is going to happen. I feel it in other people, and I see it. When I close my eyes I see the sky is dark. It's not black, it's like it is just before dawn. There is darkness, but you can see. The wind is blowing, it must be blowing two hundred miles an hour. Trees and houses are pitching over. I'm watching this, and I realize when I reach up and touch my hair that it's raining horribly. I'm seeing all this chaos and debris but my hair is not even blowing, not even wet. I'm not being affected by this. I'm just watching.

I realize that this is something that is going to take place. I meet so many people who have no checkpoints on reality. They see this world as going on forever. I know differently. From what I have been told telepathically it won't take long—within twelve or twenty-four hours the shift will be made. A lot of people will leave the planet at the time of this shift. Some people will be removed, and others will stay for the tribulations. The cycles are changing. The civilization of higher knowledge came over, driven by greed, and lost their way. With greed you lose your power as a light being and become totally human. Power misused will be the fall of human beings.

The beings who I have communicated with telepathically have told me that women will rise to take back the power and lead the way. The good news is that the world is being cleansed. I believe that where there is water now there will be land. Where there is land now there will be water. Earth is literally going to flip during this cleansing. Everything is going to be different. That is the cleansing of the world. People will have to start all over again. I think the people who will be saved from this will be the teachers. We have a Creator who will instruct the chosen few.

When my grandmother passed away I thought my world had ended. She was everything to me. I lay around for a year and looked at the sky; I wrote poetry. I couldn't believe that people could function after the death of such a great woman. When the year was up I was down to eighty-nine pounds. Everybody thought I would die. I thought I would die too. I guess I wanted to, because my world, as I saw it, had ended.

◼ *Medicine Drum*
   Shona Bear Clark, Creek

I was laying on the ground one day when the sky broke open like a big television screen. I was suddenly out of my body, hiding behind cattails. I saw a river in front of me, a great river. I could see people across the river all dressed in white, jumping and hollering underneath huge, huge trees like the redwood forest. I heard visions from all directions. There was a sandy beach in front of me and I heard this voice say, "You're in a forbidden zone. Don't get caught here."

I was hiding behind the cattails when I saw my grandmother walking down the beach. She had on a buckskin dress that was tattered and torn. She was old and hobbling. There was a canoe in the water. She stepped into the canoe and started across the river to where those people were. As the canoe glided, the wind hit her and her buckskin dress ripped off. It was gone. By the time she got three-quarters of the way to the other side she had on a new buckskin dress and looked to be seventeen years old. Her age just disappeared. I watched as she stepped out of that canoe. All the people were so glad to see her. I recognized some of them: they were her children, her sisters, and her mother. Papa was there.

She left with them through the trees. She was gone.

I knew she wasn't coming back. I knew it because she never once looked back. That was on a Thursday. I went job-hunting on Friday. By Monday I was working. I was fine. There was no reason to die. I guess she got it right. She wasn't coming back here. I can feel her in the room sometimes—her breath, her smell—but she won't be coming back. She didn't take her body with her, and I won't be taking mine.

Indian kids are taught differently than White kids. Now is the time for our teachings to be shared. For our planet. For the future of all beings.

DEVELOPING
PSYCHIC POWERS

Secret knowledge   A sign language   Inside your world   Develop psychic power   Enter a lavender light   Center yourself   In a mindful posture   Communicate with spirit   We are all connected

Send and search   Traverse the realms   At will   Go with the medicine   A temple   At the base of the skull   Rays of energy   Healing arts

Study the circle   Study the square   Study the cross   Symbols of power   Focus on long distance travel   To clear your vision   Smoke your home   With holy water   Of sage and tobacco   Breath   Your   Life Song of the Creator

Travel at will   Through time portals   Interdimensional doorways   Travel the road   The medicine way   Traverse the realms   With sentient beings   Ancestors of stars   Masters of teachers

Sweet tincture of life   A river born within   Flowing cool bitter roots of healing   Passage of growth   Cells of ancient wisdom reborn

11 THE TRUTH HAS ALWAYS BEEN HERE

Practice of Traditional Prayer

SEQUOYAH TRUEBLOOD

**Protecting the Heart
of Mother Earth**

*They pulled out our leaves
Took out our branches
Cut away our trunk
But could not touch our root
And since it's there
Our strength returns*

THE KOGI (ELDER BROTHER)

As I was completing this manuscript I was given a basket from the Kogi, the Elder Brother, through the hands of Sequoyah Trueblood. The Kogi have issued an urgent warning that high in the Sierra Nevada de Santa Marta the mountain earth is drying up. The source of water that flows to the plains below is no longer abundant. The Kogi send the message that the earth is dying, and when the earth dies, we all die.

I placed the rock with the face of the Little People in the basket of universal abundance to guide me. The new age of the Sixth World is a way of peace. We all have the choice to arrive at the door and usher in the next cycle on our precious Mother Earth. With the teachings, the instructions of our original life path, we all can prepare.

I have decided to create an institute, In the Spirit of the Drum, to bring Indian people from all directions to share their wisdom. Let the hands of the four races come together as one hand.

Aho. —NRS

Sequoyah Trueblood was born in Stroud, Oklahoma. His father is Choctaw/Cherokee/Chickasaw, his mother German/English. Sequoyah grew up on a self-sustaining farm, learning to work the land to survive. He spent many years in residential boarding school, which led him into the army at the age of seventeen. As a Green Beret he was part of the Special Forces Operational Detachment "A Team," and eventually became a major. He fluently speaks Thai, Korean, and Japanese. In the service he was a code breaker for military intelligence. In southeast Asia he was involved with "Master," the development of intelligence technology.

Sequoyah is the father of five, grandfather of four, and great-grandfather of one. He lives on the Kahnawake reservation in Canada with Marilyn Kane, one of the originators of the Native Women's Association of Canada. Sequoyah has worked extensively with Indian youth wilderness programs, the Unity regional youth program for substance abuse, and Cherokee Challenge in North Carolina. He is currently creating permaculture programs in Kahnawake, Akewasasne, and Cherokee. Sequoyah shares his teaching of global unity and compassion. He is truly a remarkable being who emanates light.

My first contact with interdimensional beings was when I was a sophomore in high school. I skipped school that day and went into the fields. I was in a lot of emotional turmoil; being removed from my family at so early an age caused me great pain. I went into the woods surrounding the field and stepped over a log and found a being. He was wearing a funny straw hat. He said, "You're Sequoyah Trueblood, and everything is okay. You're being taken care of." Then he disappeared. I was shocked, but over the years many other events convinced me that I truly am being protected.

In the army I was a code breaker for the intelligence service that monitored all communications out of Mexico. At Two Rock Ranch in California we monitored Chinese communications at what is called a listening post. We could break any code they had. Breaking codes was a natural for me. Indians are good at that. We knew everyone's secrets. I had a unit that would scan all the communications, and we would tap in to them. We also did subliminal programming over these communication lines. We did this all over the world.

I'm telling you something that is classified as "top secret," but it needs to be said. Our technology now is so advanced that we are capable of creating earthquakes and weather wars. I was in southeast Asia as a member of the Green Beret's A Team. We had a saying there about

■ *Sequoyah Trueblood*
Choctaw Nation, Oklahoma

how we were supposed to help the people change: "Grab them by their balls and their hearts and minds will follow." Inflict pain—that's the way the government looked at our mission. I did not come out of that experience all right in my mind, or in my heart.

This was all part of the path that brought me to the work I'm in now. I came from perfect preparation. Having been removed from my home and put into military boarding school, I was full of fear and insecurity and I believed what every authority figure told me. Being an A Team leader on the records was just a cover for what I was doing. I actually led a group of intelligence specialists who worked in camps all along the Laotian, Cambodian, and North Vietnamese borders. We did intelligence assessments through aerial photography, gathering high-level information that we would plan missions by. The army would then dispatch an elite group of special forces. Everything we ran was approved by the White House.

I came to find out later that these missions were going into the "Golden Triangle," the land of opium. These activities we were involved with created funds for more covert activities. Congress would not approve funding for covert activities in other countries, so the CIA had to do it another way. Drugs were sewn into the bodies of dead soldiers and flown to Pope Air Force Base outside Fort Bragg, North Carolina. The drugs were traded for money. This was a chess game, part of a strategic plan to bankrupt North and South Vietnam. The government wanted that land, and now we have resorts being built there. The phone lines were going in during the Vietnam War. We did not go there to win the war. We went there to break the spirit of the people—to get the money out and to gain control, which we did. We bought up all the local currency with counterfeit money from the drug trade and took it out of the country. The money was marked so it could follow the foreign agents who received it from the drug trade.

The elders tell me I'm protected, and the truth must be told now.

It wasn't long before I had a drug habit myself. When I started to understand I was being used to further a perspective I didn't adhere to, it became clear to me I'd been totally misled.

■ *Spirit of the Sky*
Marcus Amerman, Choctaw

We were in Banmethuot, in the central highlands of Vietnam, in
the mountains. The code name for our operation was Daniel Boone.
The other code name was Prairie Fire. We went into Cambodia, sometimes into Laos, North Vietnam, and China. We weren't supposed to
be in any of those countries. This was illegal. I was a captain in charge
of the intelligence activities in Banmethuot. We were under attack all
night. When I went out the next day to search the dead bodies of the
Viet Cong I found pictures in their wallets of mothers, sisters, wives,

their children: the same things I had in my wallet. This was the turning point. Everything became so clear to me. I was sitting on the ground between two bodies of men I had killed. Here I was, killing people over a perspective I did not believe in or support. I put my weapon down. When I sat in that field crying for those dead people, a light came over me in the shape of an egg. I was told again, "Sequoyah Trueblood, you're going to be all right. You're taken care of."

It was through warfare that I came to find the way of light and peace and love. Through warfare, the light came out of the darkness and led me on the path of what I'm doing today. When I saw these beings of light, the extraterrestrials, I knew I was saved.

I stayed in southeast Asia for another couple of years; however, I never picked up a weapon again, even in combat. I knew I was going to survive, and so I would go into combat without a weapon. People thought I was crazy. I would go into the Delta by myself without a weapon. I went on assassination missions, screening missions, and reconnaissance missions without a weapon. It was like "counting coup"— going into battle but only touching the enemy. That is what I did. And no enemy soldier ever dishonored me.

At this time I was given drugs by the government—super amphetamines to keep us awake. They would make your hairs stand up on end, like antennae. Out in the jungle you could hear sounds a mile away. I was on the front line for days at a time. I was always at risk, my adrenaline flowing. The drugs saved your life, but nobody knew how they would affect you later. We didn't call them drugs; we considered them tools to help our operational capability. I was taking a handful of amphetamines every time I needed them, and to come down I took opium. We had opium in capsules. We were guinea pigs.

I left Vietnam a drug addict, and in pain. I couldn't function in the United States. I brought back two gallons of amphetamines in plastic jars. When I did not take these pills I would get paranoid, curl up into a fetal position, and basically be paralyzed. In January 1970, I was living in a townhouse with my wife and children. I got up, packed a small bag, and left. I flew home to Oklahoma, where I withdrew from drugs while staying with some Cherokee friends I knew from boarding school.

I went into the bedroom one day. I felt sick: my stomach hurt. As soon as I put my head on the pillow there was a vortex of light, like a swirling rainbow. I got taken right up and through the vortex. I was standing in a beautiful garden. It was evening, at twilight. There were bushes and a silver object, a craft. There was a being standing there, a Grey being with a large head, big eyes, and a slit for a mouth. This being, who seemed androgynous, was covered in what looked like a silvery suit, a uniform of some kind. Telepathically this being said, "I've been asked to take you somewhere. Someone wants to talk to you." I did not feel anything extraordinary about it at all. It was like going to the store to get a loaf of bread and a bottle of milk. It felt perfectly ordinary.

I went up these steps into the craft, which was sitting on legs. I sat down by a little round window. Just like that we were traveling. I saw the Moon go by; I saw the Sun and the stars go by. Then we were in a dark void. Next thing I knew I was looking down over a perfectly white city, pure white. We got down to the city. I don't know how that happened. We were just beamed down and we were on the street, walking next to two- and three-story buildings. The streets were made out of white stone. The buildings were so close together that they seemed not to be separated. I was walking with this small Grey, much smaller than myself. There were beings dressed in white. They had blonde hair; they were beautiful people with white robes that came down to their ankles. They were not even paying attention to us.

We walked through this city and ended up in this place with beautiful trees. These blonde people with robes were seated at a table there. A woman and a man were standing by. I wasn't upset. I wasn't anxious at all. This all seemed perfectly normal to me. That is when I realized I had been with these people before, and I recognized the events of my past that led me here.

As the Grey being took me to the Blonde man who was standing, I could hear the Blonde talking to me telepathically. His lips were not moving. He said, "We brought you here to let you see that all these things that have happened to you in this life are part of a training program. You had to experience these things; you know that. We are watching over you. You are here to do a specific job. You are going to experience more hard times. When you leave here you are going to have to do some other hard things, because in learning about them you can help resolve these experiences. Then you can help other people to understand by doing teachings. You will be learning all about Native roots and ceremonies that bring teachings of compassion. They help heal the unresolved pain and suffering in consciousness, and that helps Mother Earth to heal, and all the people. You are going to be teaching Indian people. It is not going to be easy for you. Just know that you come from a place of strength, and you will be able to handle it all."

I was then invited to stay there with them. As soon as I heard that all my attachments in my life came up. My wife, my children, my automobile, the house, all my friends, my job—I knew I wouldn't have those any longer if I stayed, and that was all I had. I panicked. I told them I had to go back.

It was very evident to me that they had peace and serenity there. Everything was in harmony. That is the potential for Mother Earth. There is a lot going on now on this planet. It is all serving Creation.

Just like that I was on the spacecraft with this little Grey being, and then we were back in the garden. Next thing I knew we went through the void into the vortex of light, back to the bed. I got up and felt a bit strange. I went into the living room where all my friends were, but I could not say anything to anyone. In fact, I never spoke about that experience until I was in prison.

I ended up in prison because of my addiction. I was charged with smoking marijuana. I still had access to pure heroin that was coming in from the Golden Triangle. I was a major then, with twenty years in the military in counterintelligence, but I was busted for smoking marijuana in Korea a few months after returning from my tour of duty. I was taken to Fort Leavenworth, Kansas, where I received my dismissal papers.

They were throwing me out of the army, at least administratively.

I drove to a motel in Missouri and called a lawyer I knew. He had a friendship with a federal judge in Waco. The judge told me I could not be thrown out of the military like that, and he put a restraining order on the army. No federal judge had ever done that before; up until then federal judges had always let the army execute its own decisions without interference. The army was irate about the judge's order. I was told to stay in the motel until the commanding officer at Fort Leavenworth received the restraining order. As it turned out, since they wouldn't let me work I was on a leave of absence, in limbo, for one year, with a major's salary. Eventually I went to Austin, Texas, to work with my attorney.

There are beings, you see, watching over me. I know that now. The extraterrestrials, these beings—the Blondes—had a hand in all of this as part of my training.

On the day of my hearing I put on my military uniform and went into the courtroom. I was the only one who got to speak. There were generals from Washington acting as prosecutors, but the judge would not let them ask any questions. I spoke, and then the judge issued a temporary restraining order, which meant the military could not put me out of the service until the judge decided what to do. A general jumped up and said, "That's impossible!" And the judge said, "I'll show you how possible it is. I'm making it permanent, as of right now!"

So I went back to Leavenworth still in the army. They put me to work with very little responsibility. Then I got a call from Fort Bragg, North Carolina, from friends of mine in covert activities. I went down to North Carolina and got involved in drug trafficking. Heroin and cocaine were still coming in to Fort Bragg, and I became a pick-up boy.

The operation worked as follows. The money from the drugs went to buy arms on the open market, so it couldn't be traced. The arms went to Dade County, Florida, to someone I was on reconnaissance with in southeast Asia. He packaged the arms, which then went to Saudi Arabia and from there got sent to Iran, so the hostages would not be released and Jimmy Carter would not get credited for it. Reagan would receive credit for the hostages' release, after he was inaugurated. The arms were sent to Iran to create that scenario.

I was working for operations in 18th Airborne Core at Fort Bragg, still a major in military intelligence. My primary job was to make sure our rapid deployment force could be ready for combat anywhere in the world within eighteen hours. I was sitting in an office with cocaine in a nasal spray bottle going up my nose every thirty minutes. I was out of it. The 18th Airborne Core was affectionately called the "jumping junkies."

Well, eventually I got turned in. Someone made a deal with undercover agents, and I was arrested. It was the best thing that could have happened for me, really. I said, "Thank you, Creator." I was dying. I couldn't get off the drugs.

I was put in jail for six months in Fayetteville, North Carolina, without bond. I was tried by the government. I got three years in Leavenworth; I lost my benefits and retirement pay after twenty-one years of service. I couldn't testify in court about what was going on. I had no defense, none whatsoever.

I got dismissed from the army with two eight-year sentences, back to back—sixteen years. The judge wanted the names of the people involved in the drug-trafficking trade, but I had already been visited and threatened. I told the judge "No," and he said he could give me sixty years. The next trial was two weeks later. They gave me two ten-year sentences and one five-year sentence. Now I had sixteen years plus twenty-five; I was up to forty-one years.

The CIA came and told me that if I kept my mouth shut I would not do any time in North Carolina. I was not to talk about the arms or the drugs. I was flown in by private airplane and went to prison in a limo. I was in the drug treatment program at Fort Leavenworth prison, and I was able to kick the addiction. I got my B.A. in science from the State University of New York while in prison there. I learned a new way. I learned to meditate deeply in prison, and I learned acceptance.

I became a true helper, and stopped judging people. I began to live in peace.

Twenty-two months into my sentence they told me I was ready to get out. I was clear.

The day I left prison the sheriff from Leavenworth County was outside the door. He put handcuffs on me and chains around my ankles. He took me down to the Leavenworth County jail. I wanted to protest this, to file a writ against the extradition. He said, "Not you. The people from North Carolina will be here tomorrow."

I was put in the cell and finally spoke to the judge, who released me to the state of Kansas on $10,000 bond. The next month I had an extradition hearing, which was postponed until the next month. That went on for one year. I was on a one-month reprieve for one year. I received a letter during this twelve-month stay of my legal situation from the governor of Kansas, inviting me to Topeka, to a governor's hearing for my case. The governor and his attorney wanted me to tell them what had happened. I told them what I am saying now—I was tired of keeping everything inside. I told them they could do what they wanted with the information. I told them everything. They asked me what my plans were for the future. I actually did not know. I thought maybe I'd go to university to study psychology.

I met a healer, Jose Silva, from Mexico. He teaches healing through meditation and has many followers. It was not long before I became a teacher of meditation. This is where we get in touch with the healing force that exists in consonance with Mother Earth's heartbeat: total healing, no disease. I have not been to a doctor in over forty years. I haven't needed to.

I stayed in Kansas and started a consultation firm called A Better Tomorrow. The purpose of my work was to help people look inside themselves and help them heal; to practice meditation and prayer; to be loving, gentle, and kind; to forgive people. That is when I went to

White Cloud, Kansas, where the Sac-N-Fox Indian people are. This is where I experienced my first sweatlodge. I knew right then that that was what I was supposed to be doing. I did not know how it would all unfold, but I was on the path. I started to learn the teachings of the Sac-N-Fox people, who are a sub-band of the Lakota. I stayed there doing this work for four years, from the time I got out of prison in 1981 until 1985.

I went to my office one day and my secretary said that a couple of guys in suits had been in asking questions. I knew they were following me. These two men in suits had also shown up at my house asking my friend if he was Sequoyah Trueblood and asking for identification. They told him they had a warrant for my arrest. I had my lawyer call the sheriff's office. There was no warrant. I knew these men were bounty hunters, hired by the office of the governor of North Carolina to take me back there to do more time for drug trafficking. Kansas had given me full asylum, with a letter stating that I was found not guilty on the original marijuana charge.

I was working with the head of Clinic Masters, Gordon Heuser. When I walked out of his house I was engulfed in floodlights. Two police officers walked up to me and said, "Have you ever been in trouble with the law?" I said, "Yes." They pulled their guns and said, "You are under arrest for being a fugitive." But I wasn't a fugitive. The government had taken me out of North Carolina. I did not run from anything. Since my meeting with Gordon Heuser had been in Missouri, across the state line, the bounty hunters had gone to the local police there. They got me and took me to jail. They set up a hearing for my extradition, and the judge gave me a $20,000 bond. Gordon Heuser paid my bond, and I went back to Kansas.

Two weeks later my lawyer called to tell me that the governor of Missouri wanted to set up the same deal with me that the governor of Kansas had. I went to the courthouse in Independence, Missouri, took the elevator upstairs, got off, and the sheriff put handcuffs on me. It was a ruse. They had lied to my lawyer to trick me into going to the courthouse. A federal judge tried to block my extradition to North Carolina. The Veteran's Administration also wrote a letter on my behalf, saying that I was a combat veteran from Vietnam, that I was a Green Beret, that I had posttraumatic stress disorder and was prone to flashbacks. They went on to say I could be a danger to myself and others, and I should not be in jail.

So they put me in solitary confinement in a Missouri county jail. I was a vegetarian so I wouldn't eat the food. I fasted for twenty-one days. They thought I was going to die, so they called the psychiatrist from the Veteran's Administration. I told the psychiatrist that if I died, that was okay, but I was not going to eat that food. After that I got a vegetarian diet.

This is my life; this is what those beings told me I was going to go through. Nothing scares me.

So there I was in solitary confinement. Six months went by. F. Lee Bailey took my case and said he was going to sue the government on my behalf. He sent his staff to Missouri and they were all working with me. Investigative attorneys were questioning me, filming me for hours. Suddenly one day an associate of F. Lee Bailey's informed me that he couldn't follow through on the case. I only knew one group in America that could threaten attorneys in that way. An investigative reporter from Channel 5 in Kansas City also came and talked to me. He had statements from other Vietnam vets around the country talking about the drugs and drug trafficking.

But still, there I was in solitary. Another year went by and I was still sitting in this cell in county jail, like a monk in a cave. I got to meditate and pray every day. I was refining myself in the fire. At the end of the year the federal judge called me back and said nobody wanted the truth to come out. They were leaving me alone. While I was in there I was not a credible witness. Nobody would acknowledge my existence there. The judge told me it was up to me. I had to make the decision to go back to North Carolina on my own; otherwise I might stay in that jail forever. I knew I could die there. I had not had any sun, no fresh air for a year. So I went.

Two agents came and took me to Central Prison in Raleigh, North Carolina. In four months I was out of Central Prison and in medium-custody camp. I stayed there, in Asheville, for four or five months. Then I was sent to an honor-grade camp, close to the Cherokee reservation, where the gate was open all the time. The medicine man from the Wolf Clan, Andy Oocama, came to see me. He said, "We know about everything you have been through. You have all the qualifications to help us do an outdoor experiential program for our young people based on our culture." He became my teacher for several years. He taught me the language, the ceremonies, the songs. He got permission to take me out to the reservation in Cherokee. I met the vice-chief and all the people in youth counseling. They wanted me to do the youth program.

Sure enough, I got a call one day to go to the warden's office. I had a forty-one year sentence while I was in the honor-grade camp, but they put me on parole and let me out. They just wanted to get me off the books.

I was free. I went to the Cherokee reservation and helped build a treatment center that served all tribes east of the Mississippi River. It's still in operation. It's called Unity Youth Treatment Center. It's beautiful—in a stone building the Cherokee laid by hand. I led the outdoor program there and I also worked on the Cherokee Challenge, helping the youth understand the relationship with Mother Earth and return to the old ways. We were so successful with that program that I was asked to travel and talk about our concept and how we had implemented it. I have been traveling ever since.

I still have a home in North Carolina, where I want to grow organic food. The corn, squash—that is the medicine. I learned the plants at two years old. My grandmother took me out, and I learned the medicines by name. I still use those plants in my life, and I help people with the wild-crafted medicine. Part of my plan is to take permaculture farming to Cherokee, and also to build greenhouses.

◻ *Mother Earth*
Cliff Fragua, Jemez Pueblo

I've got Cherokee blood. There in Cherokee I got the teachings, took the sweatlodge, and finally became a leader. Just before Andy Oocama left to go to the spirit world he gave me his pipe. That is when my first pipe came, and it was a Cherokee pipe.

I started having more experiences with ETs there in Cherokee. I had been told by the Grey that they would be back to get me again. I had a house on top of a mountain. It is gorgeous there. I would walk out from my house, through the woods to this cliff, a rock cliff. That's where I'd go to pray and meditate. I was sitting there with my eyes closed one day on this mountain. All of a sudden I saw Grandmother Spider spinning the web of life. Then came this voice that asked, "How many relationships did you destroy, walking from your front porch to get out to this cliff?"

All of a sudden a light came up—there was a luminous being with iridescent wings, transparent. It was a woman, and she was beautiful—part insect, part woman/human form. I was looking right through her body, her wings. Her wings were barely moving. I was overwhelmed. Then the voice said, "We told you we would come back to get you," and she started to reach her hand out to me. Just before her hand touched my knees I said, "No! I'm not ready yet!" As soon as I said that she disappeared. I took my time going back to the house. I looked at everything I had been stepping on. What an experience that was! That was a great teaching for me.

In traveling I began working with all the tribes east of the Mississippi River. That is twenty-some tribes. I had all these teachings, from the Seminoles to the south, the Mohawks to the north, the Penobscot, the Passamaquody. All those kids were at the treatment center. I began going to Canada. I went to the Four Worlds Summer Institute at Lethbridge University, Alberta. Indigenous people from all over the world go there to share teachings.

Through that I went into the Midewiwin ceremonies with Peter Ochise. Peter's parents had kept him in the mountains of Alberta until he was forty years old. He never had western contact. Teacher after teacher would go into the mountains to give him the knowledge. He had the original water drum that was brought from the spirit world. It's kept in the ground. The water drum has been there so long that it's petrified. Peter came out of the mountains in his forties; he's eighty now. One of his primary students is George Courchene, who was with Peter for forty years. He lives in Saguine, Canada. This is Anishanabe territory, outside of Winnepeg, Manitoba. George is my primary teacher. I've learned the Bear sweat from him. I've been taught all the Midewiwin ceremonies. This is how it happened for me. Then I met William Cammanda. He took me under his wing. William Cammanda holds the wampum belts for the Algonquin people—the teachings of love, truth, peace.

These are the most important people of my path, my teachers.

I had a vision one day in British Columbia about how the universe worked in the female way. A voice in the vision told me I was to share this knowledge with Arvol Looking Horse, the pipe carrier for the Lakota/Dakota/Nakota nation, about the direction the Plains people danced. The Plains people dance into the turning of Mother Earth to resolve her pain and suffering. That is prayer. It's not like we are dancing with the Sun when we say that we have forgotten who we are. The Sun stands still in the sky; it does not turn. The Mother Earth is always turning into the Sun.

This voice told me to go to Arvol Looking Horse, who I had never met. Two months later I was standing in Arvol Looking Horse's house in Greengrass, South Dakota; my fifteen-year-old daughter was there with me. Arvol and his wife, Carol Ann Hart, have a daughter named Chante, which means "heart" in Lakota. My daughter's name is Shanti, which is Sanskrit for "peace." We had peace and the heart coming together there. I told him about my vision and we became good friends. We are brothers now.

Arvol Looking Horse invited me to come to the Sun Dance at Pipe Stone. I met the Sun Dance chief, Chris Leith, an older man. I was setting up my tepee when a man came over and told me to sit down—he was going to show me how to put up my tepee in Crow Dog's paradise. It was Leonard Crow Dog. I had already put the poles up but I hadn't put the skin on yet. It was a perfectly clear sky. All of a sudden a black cloud came out of the west and was spinning right to my poles. The cloud picked them up and threw them forty yards away! Leonard, who

◻ *Woman Spirit*
Cliff Fragua, Jemez
Pueblo

is a great spiritual teacher, gave me his poles. He built my tepee and put the skin on it. He said, "There, now that's the way we do it up here." We became good friends right then. Leonard is the one who appeared to me when I hung from a tree for my mother. I had made my harness and put it on the tree. I went out and started dancing and by the third day I had become friends with the Sun dancers there. We got along great. On that third day I pierced my skin to prepare to hang for my mother from the tree.

My teaching and knowledge have grown, and I have experienced the traditions of many Indian people. We all came from the same place, in the stars. We have the same parents in creation. In the beginning, everybody, all of our Star People, came from the same place. We are all one family. Every planet in this universe and all other universes that science doesn't know about are all populated. They are inhabited, all of them. The moment a planet starts forming from gas there is a spirit, or that gas would not be there. Then other spirits come to help maintain the flow of the energy, the forces of the elements. All these worlds are inhabited. The Sun is filled with spirits, many of them.

Native people on this Earth—we were seeded here in a bodily form. When it was time to populate this Earth many spirits came from other planets. They were here in invisible form for a long time before the bodies came. As the spirits entered the atmosphere they took on the atomic structure which formed into a body. When we exit we dematerialize the atomic structure.

We are all related, we are all family members, everyone, everywhere. We all come from the stars. We came here to this Mother Earth to do specific things, to serve Creator and creation. One of the things we are doing here, in this bodily form of spirit made visible, is working as representatives of Spirit. We are beings of light. There has been discord in the spirit world. It did not start here. We were sent here to be the arms and legs of Spirit, to interact with one another, to learn about attachments, to work through the discord.

When I speak of Spirit I mean the invisible beings, interdimensional beings, Creator's mind in motion. Anything that flows out or from the mind of the Creator is Spirit. Spirit beings live in other planes, other realms, other planets. We humans are not supposed to have full knowledge of this. We come here without it. Each one of us has a special path, and a special gift to exercise on that path. The first part of our path is through our interactions with those who we can help to heal the unresolved pain and suffering that exists in consciousness. Then we can live as the loving, kind, gentle, compassionate beings we all are, and so enjoy ourselves here on Mother Earth.

If we knew who we really were then we would never do the work. In the same manner, we never get more than we can handle. If we were given more than we could handle then some part of the mechanism of getting the job done would break down. The Star Beings are guiding us and helping us and loving us all the time. The Master Teachers—to us they are the invisible ones, grandmothers and grandfathers—they carry our prayers to Creator and, most importantly, give us the opportunities to work the answers to those prayers.

Today, for all colors of all races, the greatest hindrance is judgment. When we judge we are not fully accepting Creator's plan, which blocks the flow of healing. We must practice acceptance without judgment. Once we learn this we are protected. This is a prayer, a mantra. The symbol for this prayer is a circle with a triangle inside it. The circle is the Circle of Life, and the triangle is the heart. The heartbeat is inside that. I was given the words in Mohawk before I even knew the Mohawk language. The word for Creator is Shonkwaia' Tison—the one who fills everything, who made the bodies, who sent us here. You say that and you get used to having that relationship in your mind at every moment. We need these prayers to guide us.

At the top of the triangle appears the word Niawenhko':Wa, which is the great thanks that fills creation. After we acknowledge Creator in our lives, the next thing we must do is say thank you for everything, everything we have invited into our lives. And we must exercise free will. This is our prayer of thanks. Then you follow the Circle of Life to the left—that is the female way and that is what the whole universe is about. It is a female universe, especially here in our solar system. You follow the female way to the left bottom leg of the triangle within the circle and you come to Skennen'Ko':Wa, which is the great peace that fills creation. The only way to get to the great peace is to acknowledge Creator in everything and give thanks for everything.

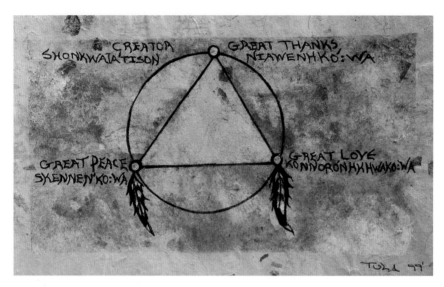

◨ *Circle of Life*
  Tula, Abenaki/Cherokee

This is the sacred geometry, the temples on top of the mounds. The circle is the female; the male is the triangle. The man comes forth from the woman. As we go around the triangle, the third corner is Konnoro'Nhk Hwako:Wa, the great love that fills creation. The only way to get there is by acknowledging Creator, giving thanks, and living in peace, where the reality of what love is becomes revealed.

Then we go back to where we started, aware of what our relationship with Creator is.

We have to experience all the negative emotions—anger, judgment, fear—to understand that we don't need them in our lives anymore. Through forgiveness and thankfulness those emotions are removed. When we give thanks there can only be forgiveness. This is a symbol, a prayer, for all the races. When you place another triangle upside down within the circle you have the six-pointed star. These symbols are records of knowledge, drawn on rocks in many sites in North America.

In the same way that the eastern people have yoga, we have a system in North America of recognizing the relationship of all things, which leads us to the path of peace. Within the petroglyphs these positions are shown. I start out by becoming the West Wind, the wind that brings the water, brings the clouds and the cleansing. Then from the West Wind I become a Waterfall; from the waterfall I become a Rainbow, and from the rainbow I become a Star Being, who becomes a star in the heavens. From a star I become a Horse. From the horse I become a Blue Heron, then Spirit taking flight. Then I become the Wolf, then the Turtle. Then I become turtle revealing itself, turning on its back, making itself vulnerable and giving itself to Creator. Then I become the Bear, then the Eagle, and then the Wampum, the shell that the wampum beads are made out of. Then I become a Snail, and then the Great Tree of Peace. Then I become a Rainbow, which is the end of the posture. I do this every day.

The terms of the Jay Treaty is only one interpretation of the Wampum Belt. Through teachings I have learned the depth of its symbols. William Commanda has several belts. He is the keeper, and several of them have a deeper meaning. What he has shown me in those wampum belts is the Law of Origin—us coming from the womb of creation, how the Sun was born and how the Sun feeds Mother Earth, and how in turn she feeds us.

The DNA is in the wampum belts. It shows when the DNA was in full bloom, when all our contact points were wide open and we were disease-free. Then it shows how we went through destruction, which is really transformation, change. Some of those points on the DNA have been shut off. Women are here to teach the men respect; they are here to bring new life into the world. When women go back to the original teachings the contact points on the DNA come back to life again. This is to resolve that pain and suffering, the time when the people turned their backs on the Creator's original teachings. That is when the DNA changed, and it has been that way until modern times. We are open to all kinds of disease because the structure of the DNA patterns was altered. Now women are altering the consciousness and the DNA is coming together again, as in ancient times.

This is all part of the prophecy in the wampum belt. Destruction becomes transformation. We are going to move through that now, in order to live here on Mother Earth in a place of peace, of love and harmony. We are going to see the reunion of all beings, of all realms, in our lifetime. It is not very far off, not far at all. Crosslin Smith has the belts for the Cherokee people, the Original People, Aniyunwiya. He lives outside Teloquoa, Oklahoma, where the Kaduwa Society has a special place. Kaduwa means "at the center." The Cherokee who were in the Kaduwa Society have all the sacred teachings and medicine for the people. Three years before the Trail of Tears they walked from North Carolina to Oklahoma. The Medicine Society took all the sacred articles and walked to the very same place the Cherokee were sent to three years later. The prophecies are all in these wampum belts.

The Cherokee, the people of the Red Star, were seeded here. They came from other planets. When the Cherokee and the Iroquois were united they built the Mound Cities, and then they migrated. The Cherokee have their clan system, just like the Iroquois. The belts give the history of the Cherokee. The wampum belts show the origin of the people, when they were united and when they came from the stars, how they were seeded and from which stars. In Cherokee they have seven clans—the Deer Clan, the Bird Clan, the Wolf Clan, the Wild Potato Clan, the Paint Clan, the Blue Clan, and the Long Hair Clan. This represents the Pleiades, the Seven Sisters. Everything is written into the wampum belt.

In early January of 1999 I found my mind being filled with a vision of traveling to a faraway land and taking the pipe that I received from the Sun Dance at Pipestone, Minnesota, in 1994. I had no idea of my destination or what would be required of me. I was sitting in Kahnawake, the Mohawk reservation in Canada on the St. Lawrence River, just south of Montreal. Kahnawake means "land by the rapids." There I was with Marilyn Kane, my wife, and we were in our house, which is essentially a healing lodge. People come there for help. I was having all these pictures in my head.

I've spent the last few years of my life trusting that I am being guided in ways that will best serve the purpose of creation. The prayers and ceremonies that I have been given are pathways of healing and compassion for creation, for Mother Earth and her children. So I was not the least bit surprised when I received a phone call from Mercedes Barrios, a Mayan woman who is a priestess. I was told that I should go to Colombia, South America, for a nine-day visit and that I was to take the pipe that I carry. There are four groups of indigenous people who live on the Sierra Nevada mountains, known as the Heart of the World.

The night before my departure I stayed in the house of John Mack. He is the head of psychiatry at Harvard University, and has interviewed me before for his books. Upon retiring I was suddenly suspended above the bed in a very open and receptive state of consciousness. The spiritual leaders of the Sierra Nevada (known as Mamas in the original language) filled my mind with their original teachings. Quite astoundingly, these were the exact teachings that I had been given over the years that I could only describe as coming from Spirit. These teachings concerned the natural Law of Origin, which governs the behavior and responsibilities of all the children of Mother Earth.

The next morning I departed with Mercedes Barrios. We went through Miami and arrived in Barranquilla, Colombia, in the midafternoon. We were met at the airport, taken directly through customs, and put on another plane that took us to a good-sized town called Valledupar. We were driven to Hotel Secarare, where a press conference had been set up to introduce the Kogi, who had arrived barefoot from the top of the mountain that morning. This was their first venture into the world of Younger Brother. The Kogi refer to themselves and the indigenous peoples of Earth as Elder Brother. The other three groups of people from the mountain were the Arockos, the Arsardios, and the Congumos.

The Kogi have the spiritual responsibility of protecting the heart of Mother Earth, to maintain her heartbeat. They do this by praying twenty-four hours a day and continually dissolving the out-of-balance thought forms that are constantly being projected into the atmosphere by Younger Brother. They came down the mountain to bring the message that Elder Brother was having a difficult time maintaining Mother Earth's heartbeat because of the ever increasing imbalance and disharmony of Younger Brothers' thoughts and behaviors.

My mind had already been filled with the information and the recommendations to Younger Brother of the help that was needed to bring our Earth back into balance. As I entered the room where the press conference was to take place I was immediately led to the center of the head table and asked to speak on behalf of the people of the Sierra Nevada mountains, the Heart of the World. As I spoke the words that had been telepathically placed in my head, the Mayan priestess stood by my side and simultaneously translated flawlessly into Spanish. The Colombian television station filmed five hours of my comments over the nine-day period. I said a prayer in closing with an eagle-wing fan, which had an oval-shaped white light around it in the film footage.

The next morning we were taken on a seven-hour four-wheel-drive adventure to the 13,000 foot level of the mountain. We were let out at the west gate of a village that was only occupied during ceremonies. There the four groups of people came together in council. We learned that the three indigenous peoples that occupied the lower levels protected the Kogi and their work on top of the mountain. The six days that we stayed at that village were spent in council with the Mamas, the spiritual leaders who came from each of the four groups. When they were in their own groups their work was entirely telepathic.

Before we were allowed to enter into council with them we were required to go through "registration." This involved us standing before the elder of the Arockos in the hot tropical Sun for five hours while he entered our minds and searched out every single thing that was stored within. Some people were rejected. We were told to concentrate on those gifts that we had brought that would be helpful to the Mamas' mission of keeping the world alive.

I became very close to these Mamas, which also is the word for Sun. Each evening I would prepare my bed outside on Mother Earth. Every night the Mamas telepathically filled my head with teachings and the awareness that they had been guiding my entire life process, that I had once lived in the village, and I was the keeper of the gate that opened to the higher spiritual realm. I was told I was to help them prepare a document outlining the Law of Origin. This document would then be delivered to the government of Colombia with specific requests. I was also told that I could speak to the press on any matter concerning them, for they were aware that I would share the correct information.

It is beautiful there, a paradise. You can walk around and pick bananas, mangos, wild beans, potatoes. You don't want for anything there. It is so peaceful—you never hear any noise. The people are beautiful. The women are the leaders. They give the men the power to speak. The stars at night are brilliant. It was, in fact, toward the end of my stay when I one night saw flashing lights moving through the sky. I saw lines of light, streaks of light going from one star to another star, connecting stars like communication travel. I was totally entranced, having never seen this before. Then I realized I was receiving teachings, personal teachings. I'm still aware that telepathic communication is my way of training there with the Kogi.

The next day we met in council to share the Law of Origin. One of the questions was, "Where did you come from? Who was there before you?" I was taken back with the Mamas. Out of the four groups of people I was the only one to be taken back with them. They stand in council and work the *porpora*—a tool for meditation. It is a gourd with an open top. The gourd they gave me is called Father of the Water. I have to carry it. This is my initiation. I keep it in the bag the Mamas gave me. When I go back down there they will cut the top of the gourd off in ceremony and put seashells that have been baked and turned into lime in the gourd. Then they pour water in, which causes a chemical reaction which is like fire. Then a stick goes in and works it. The lime comes out and goes on the cocoa leaves, which is activated by chewing. I will do that in April.

This basket is the Abundance of the Universe, and I'm going to give this to you. *[At this point Sequoyah Trueblood handed me the basket.]* Everything in the universe is in this basket. Now you have one. Now you carry the message, too, with this basket. You will go to the Heart of the Mountain with me. I'm a runner too. I will deliver the message from the Kogi to the White House. I go in there dressed like this, in white, with my sandals.

The leaves of the cocoa beat at the same consonance as Mother Earth. These are used in ceremony; they are part of the prayers. This is a natural form of cocoa; any derivative is manufactured and used as a poison by modern man. The cocoa is like the original tobacco of the Native people, which has been subverted and synthesized. There are a hundred alkaloids in the cocoa plant. Cocaine is one derivative, which is manufactured. They soak it in a solvent to get the one cocaine alkaloid out. The Kogi wish the truth to be known about what has been done to the medicine. All of the medicine of the Mother is powerful. A potato is not illegal, and vodka is made from it. Sweet flag, bear root, and calamus make the drug ecstasy. All drugs come from the roots and plants of the Mother, extracted for the purpose of profit and greed, which creates poison.

The job of the Kogi is to maintain the heartbeat of Mother Earth. I spent time with the Kogi. They don't say anything. They communicate telepathically. They are always praying to maintain the heartbeat of Mother Earth. They won't be distracted.

The Kogi came from another planet directly to here. The last night I was there they sent the pain of Mother Earth into my body. It was so tremendous that I could hardly handle it. I was screaming, and pounding on the ground. The Mother was telling me what was being done to her. I felt a tremendous pain and suffering, so unbearable I almost could not take it. She told me that some of the Elder Brothers, the Red man, were participating in forming a cancer around her breast, and that it was blocking the milk gland. The milk could not travel up to the breast to feed her children any more. The message of the Mamas is to move back into the Law of Origin or Mother Earth will die. Television, elec-

◾ *Spirits Soaring*
Michael Naranjo,
Santa Clara Pueblo

tronics, technology are distracting us from praying for Mother Earth and helping her to live. Younger Brother is destroying the world, and Elder Brother is trying to hold it together.

I'm returning in April to participate in a four-day ceremony in which I will not eat, drink, or sleep as the Mamas come before me twenty-four hours a day, continuing the teaching process that I'm to undergo. I'll come back to the United States in July for Sun Dance, then in September I will return to stay with them for one year. I'll be coming out periodically to bring specific teachings.

The Law of Origin is called the Womb of Creation; it was sent forth into matter to serve creation. The first thing that came out was light, both male and female. All the strains of DNA were connected. There were eight female and eight male strains, interconnected. Then the light and the heartbeat that was inside became the Sun. The Sun had nine children, which are the planets in the solar system. The nine planets in the solar system were lined up and turning, with the DNA— the light—all around them to hold them together, like a spider's web.

Right in the middle is the heart of Mother. Everything we do here is affecting those other children of the Sun; we are equally affecting all the other planets. Native people are underneath with braces, holding up the nine worlds. The Red people. The Kogi never wrote this before. We drew it for everyone to see. The Kogi are traveling back to these planets at night. They are in council with the inhabitants of the other planets of our solar system. I saw them come back to the atmosphere in flashes of light.

They told me that my name, Sequoyah, means "pig's leg" in my language, one who supports. I did not know this. They showed how we as Indian people are holding the worlds up.

Anything that does not support this Law of Origin, the heartbeat of Mother Earth, will be eliminated. If we don't take care of her we can't live here. Mother Earth, to protect herself, has dropped her heartbeat. In Aluna, the Womb of Creation, the heartbeat of the Sun and the Mother Earth is slowing down. The people who are in tune with her, in prayer and meditation, their heartbeats have slowed down. We are still in tune with her. The people who are in tune with technology, their heartbeats are speeding up. Right now the people in touch with the old ways—the prayers, the ceremonies, the traditions, the relationship with Earth—are protected. A loving mother never abandons her children who are obedient.

The Mamas say the world will not end. The cleansing that is already in progress will continue, but will only directly affect those people whose brainwaves and heart frequencies are tuned too far beyond Mother Earth's heartbeat. I've been given a simple way to explain this to the Western mind—great thanks, great peace, great love.

PRACTICE OF
TRADITIONAL PRAYER

Gather together   Maintain the heartbeat   Of Mother Earth   Lower the pulse   Say a prayer   Call to her   ALUNA   Breath of life   Creation   Pulse of life   Pollen   Feeding   All the children   Nursing at her breast

She is the Woman of All   The abundance   She is the leader   The universe   A basket for you   A teaching for you   The Mamas   Gather your seeds   Dance in the circle   Follow the road   The pollen road   The road of creation

Earth's children have her smell   Nature will teach   Follow the women   Weaving   the   course   Caretaking   the   planet   Nuture the earth   Grow seeds   Part of our daily prayers   Corn   Beans   Squash   Ceremonial tobacco   Share the seeds

Sing with her   Dance with her   Pray with her   Gather to harvest her gifts   Return them to her   How do her gifts taste to you?   Bursting like the seeds of a pomegranate   Her succulent nature   Spills into your bloodstream   Washing your spirit clear   Her harvest juice returns to you   Seeds of sprouts   Roots of plants   Blossoms to flower   Fruits to gather

Follow the Corn Mother   And her grandchildren   Her great-grandchildren   On the pollen road

Walk in the path   Of the illumination   Stand in the light   Of the awakening   Calling all sentient beings   A prayer   Great thanks   Great peace   Great love

THE ARTISTS

Marcus Amerman
P.O. Box 22701
Santa Fe, NM 87502

Shona Bear Clark
223 N. 12th Street
Muskogee, OK 74401
918-687-8547

Jim Farris
P.O. Box 122
Cherokee, NC 28719
828-497-4662

Cliff Fragua
Singing Stone Studio
P.O. Box 250
Jemez Pueblo, NM 87024
505-892-6516

Huga (Joe Dana)
P.O. Box 128
Old Town, ME 04468
207-827-6493

Armond Lara
544 Agua Fria
Santa Fe, NM 87501
505-820-2234

Athi-Mara Magadi
1954 Hano Road
Santa Fe, NM 87505
505-986-0326

Marion Martinez
P.O. Box 105
Glorietta, NM 87535
505-984-2795

Michael Naranjo
P.O. Box 747
Española, NM 87532
505-753-6162

Stan Neptune
P.O. Box 128
Old Town, ME 04468
207-827-6493

Duane O'Hagan
c/o Rebecca Moyer
P.O. Box 221
Arroyo Hondo, NM 87513
505-776-1272

Nancy Red Star (Tula)
In the Spirit of the Drum Institute
PMB 225, 551 Cordova Road
Santa Fe, NM 87501
505-776-5038

Hand-pulled caligraphs of Na'Ku'Set, Mother Crop Circle, Tibetan word for Ohio, and Mayan Serpent Wisdom (The Sky at Noontime).

Oscar Rodriguez
c/o Waterside Productions
2191 San Elijo Avenue
Cardiff-by-the-Sea, CA 92007
760-632-9190

Alan Syliboy
Red Crane Studios
P.O. Box 492
Truro, Nova Scotia, Canada
902-893-7825

Alex Ward
301 English Avenue
Monterery, CA 93940
408-333-1411

INDEX

Page numbers in *italics* indicate illustrations.